# Community Engagement Findings Across the Disciplines

# Community Engagement Findings Across the Disciplines

## Applying Course Content to Community Needs

Edited by
Heather K. Evans

ROWMAN & LITTLEFIELD
Lanham • Boulder • New York • London

Published by Rowman & Littlefield
A wholly owned subsidiary of The Rowman & Littlefield Publishing Group, Inc.
4501 Forbes Boulevard, Suite 200, Lanham, Maryland 20706
www.rowman.com

Unit A, Whitacre Mews, 26-34 Stannary Street, London SE11 4AB

British Library Cataloguing in Publication Information Available

**Library of Congress Cataloging-in-Publication Data**

Names: Evans, Heather K., editor.
Title: Community engagement findings across the disciplines : applying course content to community
    needs / edited by Heather K. Evans.
Description: Lanham, Maryland : Rowman & Littlefield, 2017. | Includes bibliographical references
    and index.
Identifiers: LCCN 2017019814 (print) | LCCN 2017035817 (ebook) | ISBN 9781475830828 (elec-
    tronic) | ISBN 9781475830804 (cloth : alk. paper) | ISBN 9781475830811 (pbk. : alk. paper)
Subjects: LCSH: Community and college—United States. | Service learning—United States. | Educa-
    tion, Higher—Social aspects—United States.
Classification: LCC LC238 (ebook) | LCC LC238 .C666 2017 (print) | DDC 378.1/03—dc23 LC
    record available at https://lccn.loc.gov/2017019814

To all of the instructors who bring community engagement experiences into their classrooms each semester. You have more impact in students' lives than you realize.

# Contents

# Acknowledgments

I'd like to thank the individuals involved with the Center for Community Engagement at Sam Houston State University for their work organizing events where those who incorporate service learning can get to know one another and talk about their research projects. The idea for this book came in one of those sessions. Two people who have been invaluable in this process are Dr. Joyce McCauley and Dr. Lee Miller. Thanks for letting me float the idea of this book past you, for sending out a call for chapters to your community engagement listserv, and for holding a session where faculty at SHSU could talk about ideas for chapter submissions.

# Acknowledgments

# Introduction

The idea for this book came during a meeting at my university with faculty from almost all departments about the research they were conducting in their courses that incorporate community engagement (or service learning). The purpose of the meeting was simple: get some people together who had published research about service learning and have them share their experiences with people who were unsure how to perform research on their classes. What became clear during the meeting was that while there were great studies happening at my university, very few of them had been published, and many faculty members had not thought about how to do research on the way their classes were affecting their students.

After the meeting, I approached the directors of our Academic Community Engagement (ACE) program and asked whether they thought there would be interest in putting together a book (or books) on the way faculty can study the effects of community engagement. We agreed that this project would be useful to administrators and faculty at all institutions of higher learning. Since I am at a university that takes pride in engaging students outside the classroom, these types of classes and studies are happening across all of the disciplines at my university. It was my hope that a book like this could give examples to faculty from departments as varied as Kinesiology, Sociology, and Criminal Justice.

I sent out the call for chapters and had an overwhelming response. Over 30 authors sent in their proposals, and I began to notice a trend. About half of the abstracts submitted for this book were centered on giving readers a description of how faculty incorporate service in their classes, while the other half were specifically about the effects of these classes. I decided, therefore, to propose two books to Rowman & Littlefield: one on "best practices" and one on "findings." This book is specifically about research findings.

This book provides a multidisciplinary approach to incorporating service learning in the curriculum. Various perspectives and examples are given. For instance, the first section of this volume examines students across subfields. Chapter 1 explores the effect of service learning on students at Sam Houston State University across the four years of their time there, no matter the course. Chapter 2 explores how community engagement can be used with at-risk students in a high school setting to increase their self-confidence.

This volume also includes chapters specifically about incorporating service learning at the graduate level and with online students. Previous research on service learning tends to use either high school or undergraduate college populations for study, with graduate classes being typically ignored. Chapter 3, however, gives the results of a community engagement course in victim services, and we see that students benefit greatly from community engagement in that atmosphere. Given the growth in online classes at universities and colleges nationwide, Chapter 8 gives an example of both how to engage students in an online sociology class with their communities and how to study the effects of such engagement.

For those interested specifically in the education field, Chapters 4 through 7 give an overview of how to (1) involve pre-service teachers in community engagement projects, (2) gather data on the effects of such experiences, and (3) explore ways to gather data from the community partners about their experiences in the program (Chapter 6). Two of the education-specific chapters are also about teaching to English language learners (ELLs) or English as a foreign language (EFL) learners (Chapters 5 and 7).

Finally, Chapter 9 provides readers with an overview of the research that has been performed in the kinesiology field, a field that is typically glossed over in other books on service learning.

This volume also presents multiple methods of collecting information on community engagement projects. The methods involved include interviews, case studies, reflections, and surveys. One piece also uses longitudinal data collection across four years to address the overall effect of engaging in community engagement at the beginning and end of the undergraduate college experience (Chapter 1). Both qualitative and quantitative work is included here.

It is my hope that the results in this book can be applied in whatever educational institution you find yourself. Each of the chapters presents results with different but representative student populations. In this way, the findings of this book can be applied in diverse higher education contexts. This book will also serve as a reference to administrators who are thinking about taking serious steps to link their educational mission to helping their surrounding communities.

This book presents various research findings across the disciplines in higher education about integrating community engagement in traditional course work. I hope you enjoy reading about these service projects and that you come away from this book with an idea about how to study the effect that community engagement has on students at your university.

*Chapter One*

# Community Engagement Effects Across the Disciplines

*Impacts on Political Efficacy, Engagement, and Apathy*

## Heather K. Evans

Over the past 60 years, there has been a general decline in political engagement and efficacy, as well as an increase in political apathy, especially among young people. Research has shown that dissatisfaction with politics, government, and politicians has been growing among young adults (Fox, 2014). As fewer people believe they can make a difference in politics and are thus likely to vote, those who study politics become afraid that our democracy is in trouble. With this general decline in political engagement and efficacy, there have been various get-out-the-vote (GOTV) efforts aimed at increasing involvement in politics. Lawmakers and educators alike have turned to various proposals to increase political engagement, including the incorporation of service-learning courses in the high school and college curriculum.

This chapter examines the effects of community engagement courses on college students' political engagement, efficacy, and apathy at Sam Houston State University. Using a unique data set collected at two points in time, this chapter will test whether students become more likely to engage in politics after taking a course that incorporates service learning in the curriculum and whether students become more likely to feel that they can make a difference in government.

First, this chapter presents some background information about the political engagement and attitudes of young adults. Next, the chapter will examine previous literature that ties service learning and community engagement to politics. Then the chapter will describe the longitudinal study conducted at Sam Houston State University, the key variables, and the results. Finally, the chapter will conclude with a discussion about the benefits of service learning for college campuses, as well as areas ripe for future research in this area.

## YOUNG PEOPLE AND POLITICS

As scholars have documented over the past 40 years, there has been a general decline in the voter engagement of young adults. "Young adults," defined in this study as those younger than 30, traditionally report less engagement in politics than older adults, and they report less trust in the political system and less interest in politics (Levine & Lopez, 2002; Torney-Purta, 2002). In the 2014 midterm elections, for instance, only 13% of Americans aged 18–29 voted (Edwards-Levy, 2014).

Traditionally, political science has defined a "good citizen" as someone who pays attention to politics and votes, but we do not see that holding with young citizens. As Cliff Zukin, political science professor at Rutgers University, explains, "most young people see [voting] as a choice rather than a duty. Most feel there are few if any affirmative obligations of citizenship" (Edwards-Levy, 2014). Because of these attitudes, many policy makers and scholars have been concerned about the future of our democracy.

Given this decline in political engagement, many policy makers have suggested that schools incorporate service learning into their curriculum. Service learning is a form of experiential learning where students take what they have learned in class and apply it to a real-world situation. As defined by Billig, Root, and Jesse (2005), "service learning is a teaching strategy wherein students [learn] important curricular objectives by providing service that meets community needs" (p. 3). Students traditionally perform some type of service in the community that ties directly to the curriculum, and then they reflect on it as part of the course requirements.

Many scholars have attempted to unravel the effects of these types of courses on student political engagement, political efficacy, and political apathy. The next two sections summarize those results.

### Political Engagement

One of the benefits often examined in the service-learning literature is whether taking courses incorporating community engagement increases the likelihood that students will vote or engage in politics in other ways. There are reasons to believe this should be the case. As service-learning courses require students to engage in some type of volunteerism in their communities, we should expect that engagement to spill over into politics. Many studies have shown that those who engage in their communities are more likely to engage in politics later (Almond & Verba, 1963; Beck & Jennings, 1995; Rosenstone & Hansen, 1993).

Research specifically about service learning and political engagement has mixed findings. Some studies find positive and significant effects (Billig et al., 2005; Hart et al., 2007; Levine, 2007; Nokes et al., 2005). For instance, in a study comparing high school students who had engaged in service learning to those who hadn't, Billig et al. (2005) show that service-learning students were more likely to say that they intended to vote.

On the other hand, some research shows either no effect or negative results. Using a public administration graduate course, Reinke (2003) shows that those engaging in service learning were less politically engaged than those who did not engage in the project. Morgan and Streb (2001) also show that the increase in engagement only happens for certain types of students and is dependent on the degree of ownership and voice that the students have in the service-learning project. Other work also finds mixed results (Kirlin, 2002; McAdam & Brandt, 2009).

The overall research in this area, therefore, points toward these effects, but not all studies show these effects to exist. In a meta-analysis of the literature on service learning, Celio, Durlak, and Dymnicki (2011) find that students made significant gains on civic engagement overall, however. Methodological differences may account for the variance between the above studies.

## Political Efficacy and Apathy

There are reasons to believe that students should experience higher levels of political efficacy when they are involved in service learning. A key component of service learning is trying to bring forth some positive change in one's community. If the projects succeed and students see those positive changes, it is possible that they then will begin to believe that they can also make a difference in politics (i.e., political efficacy).

The research in this area, however, has mixed findings. Wade and Saxe (1996) examined 22 different service-learning studies and show that the effects on political efficacy depend on the discipline. Some have positive results, but those are generally either about politics or the policy process (Button, 1973; Hamilton & Zeldin, 1987; Morgan & Streb, 2001; Sylvester, 2010; Wilson, 1974). Others have found no impact on political efficacy, even in political science courses (Corbett, 1977; Kahne & Westheimer, 2006; Mariani & Klinker, 2009; Newmann & Rutter, 1983). Some work even suggests that sometimes political efficacy can be affected negatively. Kahne and Westheimer (2006) show that when students engage in projects that fail to affect their communities, levels of student political efficacy decline.

When it comes to political apathy, there is very little work specifically in this area. Most of the studies on the political benefits to using service learning in the curriculum revolve around political engagement. Western Michigan University, however, lists a decrease in political apathy as one of the benefits for their students engaging in service learning (http://wmich.edu/servicelearning/students). Some studies examine political interest (Galston, 2007; Keen & Hall, 2008; Niemi & Junn, 1998), and there is disagreement about the effects there as well. While some suggest that taking a service-learning course can increase political interest (Keen & Hall, 2008), others suggest that service learning is not "a miracle cure for students' political apathy [or] civic disengagement" (Hunter & Brisbin, 2000, p. 626).

## Method

The goal of the following analysis is to determine what impact service learning has on political engagement, efficacy, and apathy. All of the studies to date usually examine limited variables and explore one classroom setting (sometimes with a control group). It is one thing, for instance, to examine whether community engagement affects political engagement in a political science course, but quite another to see these effects in a business administration course. Are the effects of service learning extended across disciplines?

Furthermore, most of the studies performed in this area examine students at one point in time. Longitudinal data collection is time consuming and expensive. Without longitudinal data, scholars are left to look at indicators of political engagement across a single semester. While some examine a test and control group to see whether their results are robust, even in those situations it is difficult to control for the predispositions of students enrolling in courses that involve community engagement.

This chapter employs the use of longitudinal data that was collected at two points in time at Sam Houston State University. SHSU is a typical large public university that serves a very ethnically and racially diverse student body. The students who attend also come from modest financial backgrounds. Data were collected from these students during orientation before they began their freshman year of college and then at the end of their tenure at SHSU.

The first round of the data collection involved asking students about their predispositions toward politics and their service and club activities before stepping foot on campus (N = 878). Four years later, these same students were given the same questions about their attitudes toward politics and the political system, and they were asked questions about the courses they took that involved community engagement (N = 150). The results that follow are from the students that completed both rounds of surveys (N = 150).

### Independent Variables

At SHSU, students can enroll in Academic Community Engagement (ACE) courses that "combine community engagement with academic instruction" (http://www.shsu.edu/academics/ace). Typically students in an ACE course perform community engagement that is connected to the course content and then reflect on their experiences. This is the essence of service learning.

To measure whether students had been engaged in some type of service-learning course throughout their academic careers, they were asked whether they had taken an ACE course. If they answered yes, they were then asked to describe what activity they engaged in. The following are some examples of the service that students were engaged in:

- "In (my) Family Violence (course), I worked with nonprofit organizations that serve Montgomery County."
- "I had to do Community Service that involved helping children and the other that involved foster care."
- "I had to volunteer with senior citizens at a nursing home or do a ride-along with adult protective service."

In the analysis that follows, the variable *ACE* is a dummy variable that is coded 1 if a student reported that they had engaged in an ACE course. In the 2014 sample, 30% of the respondents said that they had taken an ACE course (N = 45).

Gender has also been shown to affect the likelihood that one will engage in volunteerism—with females engaging more often (Hodgkinson & Weitzman, 1997; Marks, 1994; Niemi et al., 2000). Other studies have also shown that race affects volunteerism rates. White students report volunteering more often (Niemi et al., 2000). In the analysis that follows, both *Female* and *White* are included as dummy variables to control for these effects (Female = 1, Male = 0; White = 1, Other = 0). Approximately 80% of the sample in 2014 was female, while 67% was White.

## Dependent Variables

Students were questioned about whether they had taken part in many political activities in both the 2010 survey and the 2014 survey. In 2010, they were asked whether they had attended a rally, signed a petition, and participated in a political blog. In the second round (2014), students were asked if they were registered to vote, voted in the 2012 election, planned to vote in the 2014 election, made a donation to a political campaign, put a sticker on their car or a sign in their yard supporting a campaign, volunteered for a political campaign, followed a candidate on Twitter, posted a response on a blog about a political topic, discussed politics on Facebook, and liked a Facebook page of a political candidate. The percentage of the 2014 sample that said that they had engaged in each of these activities is given in Table 1.1.

Each of the variables in Table 1.1 is a dummy dependent variable in the upcoming statistical analyses. If the person reported engaging in any of these behaviors, their score is a 1 and 0 otherwise.

Students were also asked how they felt about government and politics. To capture political efficacy and apathy, students were asked whether they agreed with the following statements:

- People like me don't have any say about what the government does.
- Politics is not relevant to my life right now.
- It really doesn't matter to me who the president is.

*No Say*, *Relevant*, and *President* are ordinal dependent variables with values ranging from 1 to 4 (1 = strongly agree, 2 = agree, 3 = disagree, 4 = strongly disagree).

## Findings

As shown in Table 1.1, most students in 2014 said that they were registered to vote (73.83%). Over half of the students in this sample also said that they

**Table 1.1.  Political Engagement**

|  | Yes (%) |
| --- | --- |
| **2010** | |
| Attended a rally | 11.33 |
| Participated in a political blog | 15.33 |
| Signed a petition | 24.67 |
| **2014** | |
| Donated to a political campaign | 4.73 |
| Placed a sticker on car/sign in yard | 8.78 |
| Volunteered for a campaign | 10.07 |
| Followed a candidate on Twitter | 16.89 |
| Posted a response on a blog about politics | 23.33 |
| Retweeted something political | 26.17 |
| Discussed politics on Facebook | 32.43 |
| Planned to vote in upcoming 2014 midterm election | 47.30 |
| Liked a Facebook page of a candidate | 47.33 |
| Voted in the 2012 presidential election | 52.00 |
| Registered to vote | 73.83 |

had voted in the 2012 election, and over 47% said that they planned to vote in the upcoming midterm election. Those figures are significantly higher than what actually happened in 2014. As the U.S. Census reports, only 19.9% of 18–29-year-olds cast ballots in 2014.

When we look back at the sample at the beginning, the political activity receiving the most engagement from students was petition signing. Almost 25% of the sample in 2010 said that they had signed a petition. A little over 15% had participated in a political blog, and 11.33% had attended a political rally.

Before seeing if those who took ACE courses became more politically involved, we can split out our original sample by those who ended up taking an ACE course and those who did not. By looking back at the original data, we can see whether those students who ended up taking ACE courses were already more engaged in their communities. If they were, we have a selection bias problem. As Figure 1.1 shows, when calculating a $z$-test for differences of means, ACE students were significantly less likely than non-ACE students to report that they had signed a petition. None of the other differences are significant.

When it comes to the measures of political engagement in the second round of the survey, Table 1.2 shows the bivariate relationship between those variables and taking an ACE course. Most of the percentages reported in Table 1.2 are higher for ACE students. The results also show that while ACE students do not report statistically higher levels of registration, engaging in

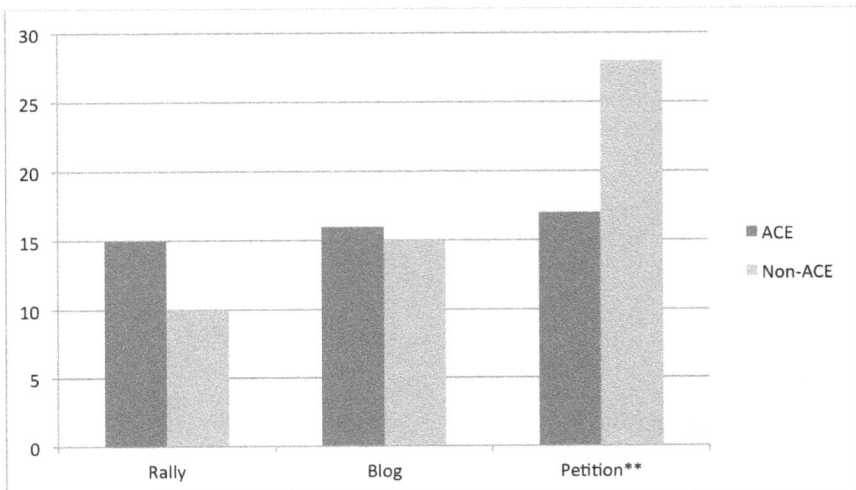

**Figure 1.1. Political Engagement in 2010**

the 2012 election, or planning to vote in 2014, four of the other variables are significant. More students engage in activities that have an online component to them (blogging about something political, discussing politics on Facebook, liking something political on Facebook, or retweeting something political) if they have taken an ACE course.

When it comes to political efficacy and apathy, students were asked three questions about their attitudes in both 2010 and 2014. The average responses to the three questions are given in Figure 1.2. As the results show, students who eventually took an ACE course reported lower levels of political efficacy in 2010 than those who did not engage in such courses. In 2014, however, they reported significantly higher levels of political efficacy than those who did not engage in service learning. ACE students were more likely to also say that they cared about who the president is and to believe that politics is relevant to their lives.

To see whether these results affect the likelihood of engaging in these activities relative to other variables (gender and race), models were calculated and are reported in Tables 1.3 and 1.4. All of the participation variables were used as dummy variables in logit models, while the efficacy and apathy variables were used in ordered logistic regression.

The results from Table 1.3 show that when other variables are taken into account, ACE is not a significant predictor of engaging in any political activities. Gender is a significant predictor of making a donation to a political candidate and following someone on Twitter, while race is a significant predictor of retweeting something political. Women were less likely to make

**Table 1.2.   Political Engagement in 2014**

|                      | ACE (%) | Non-ACE (%) |
|----------------------|---------|-------------|
| Registered           | 77      | 72          |
| Vote 2012            | 58      | 50          |
| Vote 2014            | 53      | 45          |
| Campaign             | 11      | 10          |
| Donation             | 2       | 6           |
| Sticker              | 13      | 7           |
| Blog**               | 31      | 20          |
| Like Facebook**      | 51      | 46          |
| Discuss Facebook**   | 38      | 30          |
| Retweet**            | 31      | 24          |
| Follow Twitter       | 18      | 17          |

*Note:* $**p \leq 0.01$, $z$-test

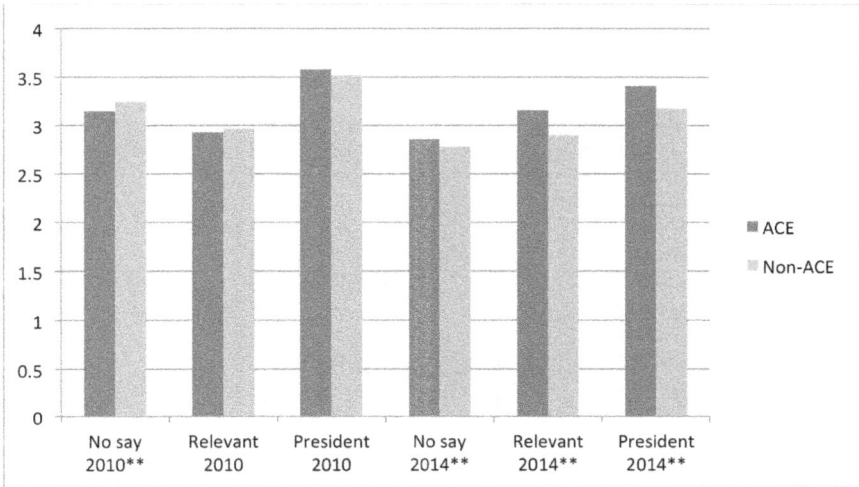

**Figure 1.2. Political Efficacy and Apathy in 2010 and 2014**

a donation or follow a political candidate on Twitter, while White students were less likely than minority students to retweet something political.

Table 1.4, on the other hand, shows that taking an ACE course is a significant predictor of political efficacy. Those who have taken an ACE course were more likely to disagree with the statement "People like me don't have any say about what the government does." Gender and race were not significant predictors of any of the efficacy and apathy variables.

**Table 1.3.   Logit Model for Political Engagement in 2014**

| | Registered | Vote 2012 | Vote 2014 | Campaign | Donation | Sticker | Blog | Like Facebook | Discuss Facebook | Retweet | Follow Twitter |
|---|---|---|---|---|---|---|---|---|---|---|---|
| ACE | 0.28 | 0.39 | 0.38 | 0.10 | -1.16 | 0.70 | 0.58 | 0.17 | 0.32 | 0.41 | 0.07 |
| | (0.50) | (0.36) | (0.37) | (0.59) | (1.11) | (0.60) | (0.41) | (0.36) | (0.38) | (0.41) | (0.49) |
| Female | -0.58 | 0.24 | 0.12 | -0.85 | -1.83* | -1.09 | -0.55 | -0.42 | -0.20 | -0.70 | -1.06* |
| | (0.28) | (0.58) | (0.43) | (0.60) | (0.81) | (0.60) | (0.47) | (0.43) | (0.45) | (0.47) | (0.51) |
| White | -0.50 | -0.51 | -0.30 | 0.19 | 0.87 | -0.08 | -0.23 | 0.41 | 0.13 | -0.95* | -0.74 |
| | (0.42) | (0.36) | (0.36) | (0.62) | (1.12) | (0.64) | (0.42) | (0.36) | (0.39) | (0.40) | (0.46) |
| Constant | 1.79** | 0.12 | -0.12 | -1.72* | -2.22+ | -1.75* | -0.79 | -0.09 | -0.76 | -0.01 | -0.33 |
| | (0.61) | (0.49) | (0.49) | (0.73) | (1.16) | (0.75) | (0.54) | (0.49) | (0.53) | (0.52) | (0.57) |
| Pseudo $R^2$ | 0.02 | 0.02 | 0.01 | 0.02 | 0.13 | 0.05 | 0.02 | 0.01 | 0.01 | 0.05 | 0.04 |

*Note:* ** $p \leq 0.01$, * $p \leq 0.05$, + $p \leq 0.10$. Standard errors are given in parentheses.

## Discussion

These results indicate that service learning, measured by whether students at Sam Houston State University had taken an Academic Community Engagement (ACE) course during their college careers, increases levels of political efficacy. At the beginning of the data collection, students who eventually engaged in ACE courses actually had significantly lower levels of political efficacy than those who did not take such courses during their time in college. At the end of the data collection, ACE students had significantly higher levels of political efficacy.

While those taking service-learning courses at SHSU report more political activity online and lower levels of political apathy, when additional statistical controls for race and gender are included in multivariate models, the effects are not significant.

There are many encouraging aspects about this study. First, the sample is longitudinal, which is generally not the case for other work in the service-learning field. This study has variables for these political indicators (engagement, efficacy, and apathy) before the students are ever exposed to the service activities.

Second, these results hold across disciplines. Many of the previous studies that focus on political variables draw their samples from political science courses or those that deal with public policy. By 2014, only one course in the Political Science department (which also houses the MPA program) at SHSU had incorporated a service-learning project, and it was at the graduate level.

**Table 1.4. Logit Model for Political Efficacy and Political Apathy in 2014**

|  | No Say | Relevant | President |
|---|---|---|---|
| ACE | 0.55[+] | 0.20 | 0.51 |
|  | (0.34) | (0.33) | (0.36) |
| Female | -0.14 | 0.12 | 0.42 |
|  | (0.41) | (0.40) | (0.42) |
| White | 0.03 | -0.18 | 0.37 |
|  | (0.33) | (0.33) | (0.35) |
| /cut1 | -1.91 | -2.29 | -1.61 |
|  | (0.51) | (0.52) | (0.52) |
| /cut2 | -0.92 | -0.43 | -0.71 |
|  | (0.48) | (0.47) | (0.50) |
| /cut3 | 0.57 | 0.97 | 0.62 |
|  | (0.48) | (0.48) | (0.49) |
| Pseudo $R^2$ | 0.01 | 0.00 | 0.01 |

*Note:* [+] $p \leq 0.10$. Standard errors are given in parentheses.

That means that these students were not engaging in ACE courses in their political science/public administration courses. Political efficacy levels are being affected across disciplines.

On the other hand, the sample in this study, while very useful, is also fairly small. Future work should examine larger samples if possible. By having a larger sample, students' attitudes and behaviors could be examined by major and specific ACE courses to see if certain courses are having larger effects on political efficacy. Future work should also examine the amount of time students spend on their service projects as well as whether they are allowed to pick the projects themselves. Some work suggests that students who engage in projects that require more time gain more political knowledge (Hamilton & Zeldin, 1987), which could possibly spill over to political efficacy measures as well.

It is also possible that the levels of political knowledge, efficacy, and apathy students have at the beginning of this study influenced just how much their attitudes changed after taking a course with a service-learning aspect. For instance, those with very low levels of political efficacy in the beginning may have made bigger gains in political efficacy than the cumulative data shows here. Unfortunately, due to the size of my sample, I am unable to test that theory here.

Finally, future work should see how long these effects last. This study shows that gains are made for many of these variables in a positive direction, but are those gains temporary? To see if this is the case, another wave of data collection would need to take place after these students graduate.

Overall, however, these results show one of the very positive side effects of incorporating service learning in the curriculum. Service learning raises the levels of political efficacy among college students, no matter the discipline.

## REFERENCES

Almond, G. A., & Verba, S. (1963). *The civic culture.* Princeton, NJ: Princeton University Press.

Beck, P. A., & Jennings, M. K. (1995). Family traditions, political periods, and the development of partisan orientations. *Journal of Politics, 53,* 742–763.

Billig, S., Root, S., & Jesse, D. (2005). *The impact of participation in service-learning on high school students' civic engagement* (CIRCLE Working Paper 33). Available from http://www.civicyouth.org/PopUps/WorkingPapers/WP33.Billig.pdf.

Button, C. (1973). The development of experimental curriculum to effect the political socialization of Anglo, Black, and Mexican American adolescents. *Dissertation Abstracts International, 33,* 4787A–4788A.

Celio, C. I., Durlak, J., & Dymnicki, A. (2011). "A Meta-analysis of the impact of service-learning on students." *Journal of Experiential Education, 34*(2), 164–181.

Corbett, F. C. (1977). *The community involvement program: Social service as a factor in adolescent moral psychological development.* Unpublished doctoral dissertation, University of Toronto, Ontario, Canada.

Edwards-Levy, A. (2014, 21 November). Millennials really don't think everybody should vote. *The Huffington Post*. Available from http://www.huffingtonpost.com/2014/11/21/young_voters_n_6200852.html.

Fox L. (2014, 29 April). Few millennials plan to vote in (2014). *U.S. News and World Report*. Available from http://www.usnews.com/news/blogs/ballot-2014/04/29/few-millennials-plan-to-vote-in-2014.

Galston, W. A. (2007). Civic knowledge, civic education, and civic engagement: A summary of recent research. *International Journal of Public Administration, 30*(6–7), 632–642.

Hamilton, S., & Zeldin, S. (1987). Learning civics in the community. *Curriculum Inquiry, 17,* 408–420.

Hart, D., Donnelly, T. M., Youniss, J., et al. (2007). High school community service as a predictor of adult voting and volunteering. *American Educational Research Journal, 44*(1), 197–219.

Hodgkinson, V. A., & Weitzman, M.S. (1997). *Volunteering and Giving Among Teenagers 12 to 17 Years of Age*. Washington, DC: Independent Sector.

Hunter, S., & Brisbin, R. A., Jr. (2000). The impact of service learning on democratic and civic values. *PS: Political Science and Politics, 33*(3), 623–626.

Kahne, J., & Westheimer, J. (2006). The limits of political efficacy: Educating citizens for a democratic society. *PS: Political Science and Politics, 39*(2), 289–296.

Keen, C., & Hall, K. (2008). Post-graduation service and civic outcomes for high financial need students of a multi-campus, co-curricular service-learning college program. *Journal of College and Character, 10*(2), 1–15.

Kirlin, M. (2002). Civic skill building. *PS: Political Science and Politics, 33,* 623–626.

Levine, P. (2007). *The future of democracy: Developing the next generation of American citizens*. Lebanon, NH: University Press of New England.

Levine, P., & Lopez, M. H. (2002). *Youth voter turnout has declined, by any measure* (CIRCLE Fact Sheet). Available from http://civicyouth.org/research/products/Measuring_Youth_Voter_Turnout.pdf.

Mariani, M., & Klinkner, P. (2009). The effect of a campaign internship on political efficacy and trust. *Journal of Political Science Education, 5*(4), 275–293.

Marks, H. M. (1994). The effect of participation in school-sponsored community service programs on student attitudes toward social responsibility. Ph.D. diss. University of Michigan.

McAdam, D., & Brandt, C. (2009). Assessing the effects of voluntary youth service: The case of teach for America. *Social Forces, 88,* 945–970.

Morgan, W., & Streb, M. (2001). Building citizenship: How student voice in service-learning develops civic values. *Social Science Quarterly, 82*(1), 154–169.

Newmann, F., & Rutter, R. A. (1983). *The effects of high school and community service programs on students' social development*. Madison: Wisconsin Center for Education Research.

Niemi, R. G., Hepburn M.A., & Chapman, C. (2000) Community service by high school students: A cure for civic ills? *Political Behavior* 22(1): 45–69.

Niemi, R. G., & Junn, J. (1998). *Civic education: What makes students learn?* New Haven, CT: Yale University Press.

Nokes, K. M., Nickitas, D. M., Keida, R., et al. (2005). Does service-learning increase cultural competency, critical thinking, and civic engagement? *Journal of Nursing Education, 44*(2), 65–70.

Reinke, S. J. (2003). Making a difference: Does service-learning promote civic engagement in MPA students? *Journal of Public Affairs Education, 9*(2), 129–138.

Rosenstone, S., & Hansen, J. M. (1993). *Mobilization, participation, and democracy in America*. New York: Macmillan.

Sylvester, D. E. (2010). Service learning as a vehicle for promoting student political efficacy. *Journal for Civic Commitment, 16*(1), 1–10.

Torney-Purta, J. (2002). The school's role in developing civic engagement: A study of adolescents in twenty-eight countries. *Applied Developmental Science, 6*(4), 203–212.

Wade, R., & Saxe, D. W. (1996). Community service-learning in the social studies: Historical roots, empirical evidence, critical issues. *Theory and Research in Social Education* 24: 331–359.

Wilson, T. C. (1974). An alternative community-based secondary education program and student political development. *Dissertation Abstracts International, 35,* 5797A.

*Chapter Two*

# Transformative Education for Students at Risk

*Intervention Through Service Learning*

Barbara Greybeck, Judy Nelson, and
Richard C. Henriksen Jr.

*This study was funded by a Learn and Serve America Higher Education grant, Engaging All Learners in Service-Learning (EASL), administered by Duke University's International Center for Service-Learning in Teacher Education.*

Within the past decade educators and researchers have expressed increasing concern about state and school district disciplinary policies that can result in stringent punitive measures and are sometimes out of proportion to the nature of the infraction. These policies have serious ramifications for the future of at-risk students, as use of the term *school-to-prison pipeline* would suggest in describing their effects (Elias, 2013; Fowler, 2011; Osher, Coggshell, Columbi, Woodruff, Francois, & Osher, 2012; Shippen, Patterson, Green, & Smitherman, 2012).

Students who have had multiple school disciplinary referrals are more likely eventually to drop out of school (Fowler, 2011) and enter the juvenile justice system (Public Policy Research Institute, 2005). Racial minorities, at-risk students, and students with disabilities are particularly impacted by zero-tolerance policies and disciplinary actions that might include suspensions and intervention by police on campus (Elias, 2013). Since behavioral infractions most often originate in the classroom, the problem should be addressed at the outset through educational interventions rather than through the segregation of students from the mainstream or through incarceration (Elias, 2013). Improvement in alternative school settings, in particular, is necessary for keeping students out of the pipeline.

Alternative education and disciplinary alternative education programs (DAEP) have been impacted by zero-tolerance policies and have resulted in increased numbers of students being housed in schools that are either in alternative settings away from the main campuses or in remote hallways within secondary schools (Fowler, 2011; Nelson, Henriksen, & Greybeck, 2016). As an example, zero tolerance for disciplinary infractions has been in place in the state of Texas since 1995 and resulted in 100,000 referrals to DAEP during the 2005–2006 academic year alone (Fowler, 2011).

Students placed in these alternative settings are caught in a downward spiral and are often blamed for their own failure (Greybeck, 2015). These programs tend to be deficit oriented rather than possibility focused (Nelson & Eckstein, 2008), and researchers have called for transformative measures to alleviate these practices (Pane & Salmon-Florida, 2009). Strategies for improvement in these alternative settings would include higher expectations and the fostering of community engagement (Shippen et al., 2012).

One type of community engagement, known as service learning, responds well to this need because of its transformative nature (MacClellan, 2009; Marbley, Malott, Flaherty, & Frederick, 2011; Nelson & Sneller, 2011). It ties together curricular objectives and community involvement through reciprocal partnerships so that students engage in real-life problem solving and reflection and are given a voice in determining the nature and direction of their work (Greybeck, 2015).

Researchers in service learning during the past three decades have found positive effects for students in the areas of academic improvement, self-esteem, civic responsibility, and motivation (Billig, 2004; Furco & Root, 2010; Scales, Blyth, Berkas, & Kielsmeier, 2000; Scales & Roehlkepartain, 2005). As such, the purpose of this project was to work with high school students in a DAEP with the hope of creating a service-learning model that would result in educational reform for at-risk youth.

At the same time, in order to quantify the effect of the initiative, the authors conducted research during the project to measure outcomes for students. Based on previous research findings regarding the effectiveness of service learning, the authors of this study hypothesized that DAEP students' self-perceptions with regard to their own academic aptitude might change after being involved in a meaningful service-learning experience.

## BACKGROUND OF THE STUDY

The students in the DAEP at this high school in Southeast Texas had been referred there for any number of behavioral problems in school and/or for criminal activity outside of school. At the time of this study, all of them were failing some or most of their eight classes and were assigned to DAEP for a minimum of three weeks. These students were housed in one classroom under lock and key at their own high school for the entire school day and were not permitted access to any other part of the building. They entered and exited the room through a rear door, and they were also not permitted to attend extracurricular activities or school functions.

While in the classroom, students were supervised by certified teachers, paraprofessionals, and police. According to the DAEP principal, small group instruction was provided by content area teachers who were assigned to work with these students on a rotating basis. When not working with teachers, students completed computer modules from the American Preparatory Institute (API) or assignments from a computer program called PLATO.

The research was carried out over one academic year by faculty and students from Sam Houston State University in Texas as they implemented service learning in this setting. The National Youth Leadership Council's (NYLC) eight *K–12 Service-Learning Standards for Quality Practice* (2008) became the cornerstone of the project and included such aspects of service learning as meaningful service, link to curriculum, reflection, diversity, youth voice, partnerships, progress monitoring, and the need for sufficient duration and intensity of the service experience (NYLC, 2008).

The STARS model (Student Leadership, Thoughtful Service, Authentic Learning, Reflective Practice, Substantive Partnerships) (RMC, 2006) was implemented with the DAEP students. This model ensured that high standards for service learning were employed. For example, students determined which project they would complete and were leaders in the project as it was planned and implemented.

Two service-learning projects were carried out by the DAEP students, one during the fall semester and one in the spring semester. In the fall, two university faculty members, four graduate students, and two pre-service worked directly with 14 DAEP students for 10 weeks during their lunch period in the DAEP facilities. On Tuesdays, students engaged in the service-learning component, while reflection about the project was conducted in small group counseling sessions on Wednesdays and Thursdays. These counseling sessions were not limited to discussions of the service-learning project, but they did serve to reinforce the activities that students did on Tuesdays.

In the spring semester, because of time constraints, the team concentrated only on the service-learning component of the project. Some DAEP students did receive counseling from graduate students, but the counseling was not directly connected to the service-learning project as it had been in the fall. Another graduate student facilitated the service-learning experience along with a university faculty member from the fall and a different undergraduate methods student. Fifteen DAEP students participated in the program for eight weeks in the spring.

The students spent ample time discussing, brainstorming, and reaching consensus on each project, and the educators ensured that the project complemented the educational goals of the students' respective grade levels. The students also had time to reflect on their service learning during the sessions with the educators as well as during their fall group counseling sessions. Lastly, the partnership between the DAEP students and the general student body was substantial in that the DAEP students would provide excellent, researched information to their peers in the mainstream population.

## DESCRIPTION OF THE PROGRAM

### Participants

Purposeful and criterion sampling (Onwuegbuzie & Collins, 2007) was employed in the selection of the DAEP participants. The criteria necessary for inclusion were (a) being a student in the DAEP program, (b) having parental permission and support to participate in service learning, and (c) having a long-term placement in the DAEP program (1–3 months).

Over the course of the academic year, 27 students in grades 9–12 were selected for the project, including two who participated in both the fall and spring semesters. The majority (57%) were African American males, while four (17%) were African American females and two (7%) were White females. The remaining students (19%) were Hispanic males. There were 14 participants from the university including five counseling graduate students, a graduate student from family and consumer science, and a graduate student from computing and information science. Four faculty members from various departments and three undergraduate methods students in teacher preparation were also involved.

The five students from the counseling department included one male student and four females, and all were Caucasian. These graduate students were studying to be licensed professional counselors, and they were enrolled in a course that was a practicum in group counseling. They were required to conduct group counseling for a minimum of 10 hours during that particular semester; therefore, the counseling that they conducted with the DAEP students met the requirement for their class. These master's level students were supervised each week by a doctoral candidate in the counselor education program who was also on-site during the counseling sessions and available to assist or intervene if necessary.

The remaining two graduate students were African American women, and the three undergraduate students were Caucasian women. One of the faculty members was an African American male, one was an Asian American female, and the other two were Caucasian females. Thus the demographic makeup of the facilitators was quite diverse.

It is important to note that quantitative data were gathered only during the fall semester, even though the service-learning project continued into the spring semester. Most of the students in the fall were exited from the program in December so that the participants changed for the spring. There were nine DAEP students who completed both the pre- and post-assessments during the fall semester, including eight African American students and one Hispanic student. Additionally, there were two female students and seven male students. The students ranged in age from 16 to 18 and were in grades 9 through 12. All of the students had been placed in DAEP at least twice, with the duration of placement from one to three months. One student had previously been placed in a state juvenile detention facility.

## Fall Semester

During weekly service-learning sessions, faculty and students from the university facilitated discussions with DAEP students about social issues in their community. These discussions led to the selection of HIV/AIDS awareness as their choice for the focus of their project. Because nearly all of the high school students in the group indicated that they knew someone with HIV or AIDS, this topic was clearly relevant and meaningful. They brainstormed ideas about the kind of project they could do, such as producing an awareness video, organizing a school awareness day, inviting a speaker to the school, or raising money for the local AIDS foundation. At length, they decided to produce a video about HIV/AIDS directed toward their fellow high school students.

In the next phase, students generated their own questions about the topic, such as, "Where did HIV/AIDS start?" "How long before someone dies from it?" and "Is it a problem here?" Then they sought answers to their questions from videos, books, and other written materials. They participated in lively discussions, and more questions were posed, such as, "What are the symptoms of HIV/AIDS" and "Do you need an HIV test in order to get married?" These questions eventually formed the basis for the information they planned to cover in their awareness video.

Students designed posters as a backdrop for their video, and they practiced asking and answering questions in order to record a panel presentation. One student was chosen to be the cameraman, and everyone approached the recording session as a professional filming event. Students were quiet during the shooting of each take, except for the student in front of the camera. One of the facilitators acted as director, working with each student on their gestures and their spoken lines before the filming began. Although not all students were video-recorded because of time constraints, it was clear that the students present during the production phase had learned a great deal about HIV/AIDS.

## Spring Semester

In the spring, with the introduction of a new graduate facilitator and a different makeup of high school students, the focus became one of support for the needs of the students themselves, rather than social issues outside of their school. During the initial brainstorming sessions, most of the students expressed a concern about the DAEP program, openly discussing their feelings about the rules and the expectations of the program. Students returning to DAEP for a second time felt they had been labeled by teachers and students as "DAEP" even after they had initially exited the program. In fact, they felt that teachers in their mainstream classrooms seemed to notice their inappropriate behaviors more than they did those of other students who were behaving in a similar way.

The students titled their project "Don't Judge Us" and began working on a video to illustrate their experiences. One student agreed to meet with the associate principal of the school to explain the project and request permission to continue. This student prepared for the meeting by writing a script and role-playing, and the project was approved. A graduate student taught the students to operate the *Xtranormal* web-based program for creating short animated productions. The students wrote scripts about situations that might result in placement in DAEP and then rewrote those same situations to illustrate how they could avoid conflict. Three laptop computers were brought to the classroom on loan from the university, and students produced three brief clips, later shared with school administrators.

The project fostered social agency among the students and a feeling of empowerment as they openly voiced their concerns about DAEP. In the process, besides the academic skills needed to produce the video, they also learned from their peers more appropriate responses to conflict. When the students complained about how teachers had initially responded when they returned to the classroom after exiting DAEP, the facilitator discussed with them the importance of finding ways to respond to teachers to avoid conflict, and then they brainstormed what they could do when these situations would occur.

The script of the first video included this scenario, illustrating a response of anger on the part of the character representing the student. In the second video, the same character ignored the teacher's negative tone and complied with her request to sit down in the empty seat at the back of the room without comment. The students stated that they learned from this discussion that it's fine to feel anger but that it's not always necessary, or advisable, to act on this anger in the moment.

At year's end, the DAEP administrator provided unanticipated evidence of the project's success. There had been fewer disciplinary referrals at the school, student attendance had improved in DAEP, and there had been almost no recidivism after students had exited the program. Additionally, almost all of the seniors in the program graduated from high school, and all but one student had either found employment or had enrolled in college.

## METHOD

Data were analyzed for pre-test and post-test comparisons using a revised version of the Academic Self-Description Questionnaire II (ASDQII) (Marsh, 1990). These data were used to identify in which academic areas students' notions of themselves as students changed as a result of the service-learning experiences. The ASDQII contains 17 scales including 9 core subject matter subscales, 6 non-core subject subscales, 1 physical education subscale, and 1 general school subscale (see Table 2.1). Coefficient alpha estimates of reliability for the ASDQII scales vary from .885 to .949 (Marsh, 1990).

### Data Analysis

Data were analyzed to determine the direction of change experienced by the participants. Scores for each student on the questionnaires were determined by summing the scores for the questions contained in each subscale and then calculating the mean score for each of the 14 subscales. The ASDQII includes a separate subscale that identifies each student's overall school self-description. Once the students' separate subscale means were determined, those means were aggregated, and an overall subscale mean was calculated. Aggregated subscale means were determined for all 14 subscales, and the direction of change was found for each of the subscales. ANOVAs were conducted on each set of subscale scores to test the significance of the differences in scores between the initial survey and the survey administered at the end of the first semester of the project.

## RESULTS

Several subscales of the revised ASDQII were used to give a broad picture of the students' attitudes both before and after their involvement in the service-learning program. Table 2.1 represents the mean score changes in students' attitudes regarding their academic subjects in high school.

Students' scores significantly improved at the .05 level in all areas except for physical education. Among the remaining categories, the area of foreign

**Table 2.1.**

| Subject | Pre *n = 9* | Post *n = 9* | Difference |
|---|---|---|---|
| Computer science | 5.391 | 5.688 | +0.297 |
| English | 5.016 | 5.598 | +0.582 |
| History | 5.014 | 5.921 | +0.907 |
| Math | 4.060 | 5.350 | +1.290 |
| Physical education | 5.879 | 5.481 | -0.398 |
| English literature | 5.166 | 5.606 | +0.440 |
| Art | 4.981 | 5.405 | +0.424 |
| Science | 5.041 | 5.580 | +0.539 |
| Music | 4.800 | 5.838 | +1.038 |
| Psychology | 4.391 | 5.974 | +1.583 |
| Industrial arts | 4.796 | 5.655 | +0.859 |
| Foreign language | 3.683 | 5.688 | +2.005 |
| Health | 4.950 | 5.683 | +0.688 |
| Overall school subjects | 4.894 | 5.839 | +0.945 |

language had the greatest difference, 2.005, while the difference in scores in the area of computer science showed the least change. Statistically significant differences in scores were seen in history, math, music, psychology, industrial arts, foreign language, and health. The difference in the students' overall academic self-definition was also statistically significant. These findings suggest that the students in general felt more positive about their own academic capabilities at the conclusion of the first semester of the program than they did at its inception.

## Implementation of NYLC Standards

Each of the eight NYLC standards (2008) was addressed in the yearlong effort as the project evolved. Facilitators kept in mind the notion of student choice and met often to debrief. Team planning became the greatest challenge.

## Standard 1: Meaningful Service

Service learning implies community engagement, but that engagement must be relevant and meaningful to the participants as well as appropriate for their developmental stage and their abilities. Because the DAEP students themselves planned their service projects, the process was at times disorganized and sometimes frustrating. Facilitators had to keep the goal of the session at the forefront, working together with students around a discussion table each week to talk about the issues they experienced in their school, their neighborhood, and society in general.

During the first semester, the choice of topic was perhaps driven more by the students' personal fear of HIV/AIDS than by a concern for community awareness. They were eager to get their questions answered, and they discovered a camaraderie among themselves as they did so. Then in the second semester, the facilitator was more open to considering the DAEP experience itself as the topic of social concern. In the quest to ensure that the project was meaningful, the facilitators discovered that for students in this type of setting, their own immediate community was the one most in need of service.

## Standard 2: Link to Curriculum

Service learning is an instructional strategy with clearly delineated learning goals and objectives. In fact, the students' learning was not necessarily quantifiable but did touch on many of the Texas Essential Knowledge and Skills (§110.30), including the following:

1. analyzing the relevance, quality, and credibility of evidence given to support or oppose an argument for a specific audience;
2. analyzing how messages in media are conveyed through visual and sound techniques (e.g., editing, reaction shots, sequencing, background music);
3. planning a first draft by selecting the correct genre for conveying the intended meaning to multiple audiences, determining appropriate topics through a range of strategies (e.g., discussion, background reading, personal interests, interviews), and developing a thesis or controlling idea; and
4. structuring ideas in a sustained and persuasive way (e.g., using outlines, note taking, graphic organizers, lists) and developing drafts in timed and open-ended situations that include transitions and the rhetorical devices used to convey meaning.

In addition, in the fall semester students worked on essential skills from the high school health curriculum (§115.31) such as the following:

1. The student is health literate in disease prevention and health promotion throughout the life span.
2. The student recognizes the importance and significance of the reproductive process as it relates to the health of future generations.

3. The student understands how to evaluate health information for appropriateness.
4. The student analyzes the relationship between unsafe behaviors and personal health and develops strategies to promote resiliency throughout the life span.

Last of all, essential skills were addressed from the social studies curriculum (§113.47, "Special Topics in Social Studies"), including the following:

1. applying social studies methodologies encompassing a variety of research and analytical tools to explore questions or issues thoroughly and fairly to include multiple perspectives;
2. evaluating effects of major political, economic, and social conditions on a selected social studies topic;
3. appraising geographic perspective that considers physical and cultural processes as they affect the selected topic;
4. examining the role of diverse communities in the context of the selected topic;
5. analyzing ethical issues raised by the selected topic in historic, cultural, and social contexts;
6. locating, analyzing, organizing, synthesizing, evaluating, and applying information about the selected topic; and
7. identifying, describing, and evaluating multiple points of view.

## Standard 3: Reflection

Students reflected before, during, and after the service projects were completed. An unusual but clearly beneficial part of this intervention was the group counseling aspect, carried out on a weekly basis on the days following the service planning. In this setting, the high school students were free to discuss their accomplishments, concerns, and wishes without fear of repercussion, and they were able to process other challenges in their lives that might have had an impact on their academic success.

## Standard 4: Diversity

The DAEP students experienced diversity in several ways. First of all, there was the layering of educational experiences of the participants, who included high school students and teachers and undergraduate and graduate university students and professors. Exposure to educational outcomes that the DAEP students may not have experienced before opened their curiosity and imagination to new opportunities. Additionally, there were racial, ethnic, linguistic, and socioeconomic differences among the participants.

## Standard 5: Youth Voice

The DAEP students were asked to identify problems of interest to them in their school environment, their neighborhood, and society in general. Student choice became a central theme as the study unfolded, and the service-learning topics emerged from lengthy discussions about social issues. Throughout the creation of the two projects, these high school students were expected to make decisions, carry out the goals of the projects, and support each other throughout the planning and implementation of the projects.

## Standard 6: Partnerships

The hope was to strengthen the partnership between the university and the high school by addressing academic outcomes for the DAEP students through the use of service-learning activities. In so doing, high school teachers were encouraged to see the value of service learning in their own teaching. At the same time, the project served as a training site for undergraduate students seeking certification as teachers and graduate students seeking counseling licensure at the university, as well as for graduate students in other fields. Because of the multidisciplinary nature of the project, partnerships were created among several university departments, including Counseling Education, Curriculum and Instruction, Language, Literacy and Special Populations, Computer Sciences, and Family and Consumer Sciences.

## Standard 7: Progress Monitoring

During the program, university students and faculty met to debrief on numerous occasions to discuss lessons and to review progress toward goals. Between the fall and spring semesters, changes were made in scheduling and in the focus of the program, partially as a result of an analysis of project outcomes in the fall semester, but also because a new high school administrator came on board.

At the conclusion of the project, faculty members met with DAEP personnel and administrators at the high school to present the students' projects and the research findings. A report was submitted to the principal, and a workshop highlighting the program was arranged for university faculty from a cross-section of disciplines in order to highlight the impact service learning could have on the quality of teaching.

## Standard 8: Duration and Intensity

This service-learning project spanned two semesters during one academic school year. The DAEP students met with the service-learning sponsors from the university for approximately one hour each week. In addition, students had time to reflect on their service and their relationships with each other, the faculty sponsors, and their DAEP teachers during a one-hour group processing session each week. As a result of this project, other faculty members from the university made commitments to the continuation of service learning at the DAEP.

## DISCUSSION

This project demonstrated that service-learning assisted DAEP students in bringing about positive changes in their self-perceptions about academic work, even though they had not been specifically taught academic content. Instead, students used skills such as reading and writing, public speaking, visual arts, inquiry, and use of technology to complete their service project. They learned concepts related to social studies, science, and health in an authentic way during the process.

The decrease in mean scores on the revised ASDQII in physical education noted in Table 2.1 could be attributed to the absence of physical education classes for students in DAEP. However, since the students' mean score in physical education was the highest of any subject area score even before the project started, the students already had a more positive attitude toward their capability in this area. Yet it should be noted that even subject areas that had little or no integration in the service-learning activities, such as music and foreign language, showed significant improvement.

Because students were given choices in their work and had learned to problem-solve to achieve a product, they appear to have gained self-confidence. They had the opportunity to reflect on their work in confidential group counseling sessions, which further supported team building and their achievement of a goal.

While this project demonstrated that service-learning pedagogy did engage these at-risk students and assist in bringing about a positive change in their attitudes about academic work, it would better function as a preventative measure rather than as a treatment option, especially in a program like DAEP. In future projects, perhaps students who are experiencing disciplinary problems can be grouped with other, less disruptive classmates in order to earn class credit for service-learning activities in hopes of preventing students' placement in DAEP.

Once students had been placed in such a program, the logistical nature of their placement affected the quality of their experiences. Attendance varied widely each session because new students were continuously being placed in the classroom, while others exited the program. There were occasional absences among students as well as expulsions from school. During each session, it was necessary to bring new or returning students up to date on what the group was doing.

In DAEP the establishment of trust between students and teachers and even among the students themselves should be a priority. In service learning, a certain amount of bonding and consensus building are also essential. Gaps in participation prevent students and facilitators from gaining this deeper level of trust and bonding. For future implementation in DAEP, projects would need to be more intensive, perhaps daily blocks (3–4 hours) over a shorter period of time, such as three weeks. In that way, momentum would not be lost and there would be less variation in attendance.

The counseling component proved to be successful with these at-risk students, but clearly addressing issues such as impulse control, anger management, and conflict resolution are valuable as preventative measures as well. The counseling sessions enabled the students to discuss issues that they perceived to be inequitable or unjust regarding school rules, teacher behaviors, and administrative decisions. These discussions, which took place in a safe and non-judgmental environment, gave students a sense of being heard and respected for their beliefs and attitudes.

When students sense that their thoughts and feelings matter, they are more likely to cooperate with school personnel even if they don't get the concessions they would like. Because the counselor trainees listened to the students, provided empathy, and acknowledged their feelings, these graduate students were actually modeling behavior that works well in any group situation such as conducting a project with others. Those behaviors were then transferred to the project that the DAEP students were organizing. Continuous counseling services at school are recommended for students with behavioral problems to avoid disciplinary actions such as placement in DAEP.

One of the most powerful aspects of this project was the interaction among multiple partners. Not only was there institutional buy-in from the university's community engagement center and from the high school administration, but faculty in various departments within the university were also integral to the success of the program. Teacher preparation students from both elementary and secondary education as well as graduate students also participated. Within the high school, every teacher attended training on service learning at the beginning of the school year, and planning was carried out with school personnel.

On the other hand, the establishment of *reciprocal* partnerships with the schools is a vital component in projects of this type. While the school administrators *approved* the project, its implementation was the sole responsibility of university personnel. Administrators were involved in the planning stages and were available for consultation, but the program would have been enhanced if high school teachers and paraprofessionals had participated with the students in DAEP in the service-learning projects. Because this was seen as a university intervention, once university personnel left the school each week, there was no follow-through until the next session.

Because of the number of institutional entities involved, the scheduling of meetings, debriefings, planning sessions, and consultations with faculty, graduate students, and administrators proved to be a challenge. Training was, and should be, required for personnel at each level as well. Although this kind of *layering* among professionals is beneficial to both university and public school students and to the project as a whole, it requires a great deal of coordinated effort.

University students were able to gain authentic understanding of academic concepts in their respective disciplines, while the DAEP students had an opportunity to learn and apply concepts in various fields with the assistance of these older peers. Still, this kind of cross-disciplinary approach requires a strong commitment from at least one coordinator at each institution who is already knowledgeable about service learning and can be compensated for the hours of extra time required to implement such a project.

University students also should be compensated with course credit for participating, and although some participated as part of course requirements, others were volunteers who simply wanted to learn more on their own about working with DAEP students. Nonetheless, depending on individuals who are willing to help out is simply not enough.

## CONCLUSION

The implementation of service learning is a process that includes more than the final outcome or product. The experiences of identifying community needs, inquiry about a selected topic, and the demonstration of an action to address a problem build attributes such as critical thinking, decision making, self-confidence, problem solving, and the ability to collaborate with others in pursuit of a common goal. These attributes are not measured on standardized tests, and yet they are indispensable for success in the 21st century. Students truly become engaged in learning and are given a voice in how this learning will proceed and how they will be evaluated.

In these projects with DAEP students, connections were readily made with curricular areas: with literacy through reading and writing activities, with technology through inquiry, with computer studies in the creation of final products, with oral language development through discussions and role-playing, with health and science through their exploration about HIV/AIDS, with social-emotional development through their counseling reflections and discussions of their own behavior, with art in the creation of posters, and with social studies in their discussions of social class and economic effects on the incidence and treatment of HIV/AIDS.

There was additional anecdotal evidence demonstrating changes that cannot be quantified for these students termed "at risk." One student applied for and was admitted to college, another took the lead in working with technology, and still others showed potential for leadership and public speaking. In short, projects of this type help to improve academic skills, build character, and strengthen bonds between the university and the local community.

## REFERENCES

Billig, S. H. (2004). Heads, hearts, hands: The research on K–12 service-learning. In National Youth Leadership Council, *Growing to greatness 2004* (pp. 12–25). St. Paul, MN: NYLC.

Byers, N., Griffin-Wiesner, J., & Nelson, L. (Eds.). (2000). *An asset builder's guide to service-learning.* Minneapolis, MN: Search Institute.

Elias, M. (2013). The school to prison pipeline. *Teaching Tolerance, 43*, 38–40. Retrieved from http://www.tolerance.org/sites/default/files/general/School-to-Prison.pdf.

Fowler, D. (2011). School discipline feeds the pipeline to prison. *Phi Delta Kappan, 93*, 14–19. Retrieved from http://pdk.sagepub.com/content/93/2/14.full.pdf+html.

Furco, A., & Root, S. (2010). Research demonstrates the value of service learning. *Phi Delta Kappan, 91*(5), 16–20.

Greybeck, B. (2015). Addressing educational equity through service-learning. In György Mészáros & Franciska Körtvélyesi (Eds.), *Social Justice and Diversity in Teacher Education: Proceedings of the ATEE Winter Conference, 15–17 April, Budapest, Hungary.* Budapest–Brussels: Magyar Pedagógia Társaság—ATEE (e-book) (pp. 95–109). Retrieved from http://ateewinter2014.blogspot.hu.

Leach, L. F., Henson, R. K., Odom, L. R., & Cagle, L. S. (2006). A reliability generalization study of the self-description questionnaire. *Educational and Psychological Measurement, 66*, 285–304.

MacClellan, D. (2009). Linking university and high school students: Exploring the academic value of service-learning. *International Journal of Learning, 16*(7), 239–250.

Marbley, A. F., Malott, K. M., Flaherty, A., & Frederick, H. (2011). Three issues, three approaches, three calls to action: Multicultural social justice in schools. *Journal for Social Action in Counseling and Psychology, 3*(1), 59–73.

Marsh, H. W. (1990). The structure of academic self-concept: The Marsh/Shavelson model. *Journal of Educational Psychology, 82*, 623–636.

National Youth Leadership Council. (2008). *K–12 service-learning standards for quality practice.* Retrieved from http://www.nylc.org/k-12-service-learning-standards-quality-practice.

Nelson, J. A., & Eckstein, D. (2008). A service-learning model for at-risk adolescents. *Education and Treatment of Children, 31*, 223–237. Retrieved from https://www.questia.com/library/journal/1G1-179048726/a-service-learning-model-for-at-risk-adolescents.

Nelson, J. A., Henriksen, R. C., Jr., & Greybeck, B. (2016). Service-learning. In R. J. R. Levesque (Ed.), *Encyclopedia of adolescence.* doi:10.1007/978-3-319-32132-5_232-2.

Nelson, J. A., & Sneller, S. (2011). Ensuring quality service-learning experiences for at-risk adolescents. *Prevention Researcher, 18*(1), 14–17.

Onwuegbuzie, A. J., & Collins, K. M. T. (2007). A typology of mixed methods sampling designs in social science research. *Qualitative Report, 12*, 281–316. http://nova.edu/ssss/QR/QR12-2/onwuegbuzie2.pdf.

Onwuegbuzie , A. J., & Leech, N. L. (2007). Validity and qualitative research: An oxymoron? *Quality & Quantity, 41* , 233–249.

Osher, D, Coggshell, J., Columbi, G., Woodruff, D., Francois, S., & Osher, T. (2012). Building school and teacher capacity to eliminate the school-to-prison pipeline. *Teacher Education and Special Education, 35*, 284–295. Retrieved from http://tes.sagepub.com/content/35/4/284.full.pdf+html.

Pane, D. M., & Salmon-Florida, A. (2009). The experience of isolation in alternative education: A heuristic research study. *Western Journal of Black Studies, 33*(4), 282–292.

Public Policy Research Institute, Texas A & M University. (2005). *Study of minority overrepresentation in the Texas juvenile justice system final report.* Retrieved from http://dmcfinalreport.tamu.edu/DMRFinalReport.pdf.

RMC Research Corporation. (2006). *K–12 service-learning project planning toolkit.* Scotts Valley, CA: National Service-Learning Clearinghouse. Retrieved from http://www.servicelearning.org/filemanager/download/K-12_Service-Learning_Project_Planning_Toolkit.pdf.

Scales, P., Blyth, D., Berkas, T., & Kielsmeier, J. (2000). The effects of service-learning on middle school students' social responsibility and academic success. *Journal of Early Adolescence, 20*(3), 331–358.

Scales, P. C., & Roehlkepartain, E. C. (2005). Can service-learning help reduce the achievement gap: New research points toward the potential of service-learning for low-income students. In National Youth Leadership Council, *Growing to Greatness 2005* (pp. 10–22). St. Paul, MN: NYLC.

Shippen, M., Patterson, D., Green, K., & Smitherman, T. (2012). Community and school practices to reduce delinquent behavior: Intervening on the school-to-prison pipeline. *Teacher Education and Special Education, 35*, 296–308. Retrieved from http://tes.sagepub.com/content/35/4/296.full.pdf+html.

Texas Education Code. (1998). §115.31. Implementation of Texas essential knowledge and skills for health education, high school. Retrieved from: http://ritter.tea.state.tx.us/rules/tac/chapter115/ch115c.html#115.31.

Texas Education Code. (2009). §110.30. Implementation of Texas essential knowledge and skills for English language arts and reading, high school. Retrieved from http://ritter.tea.state.tx.us/rules/tac/chapter110/ch110c.html#110.33.

Texas Education Code. (2011). §113.47. Special topics in social studies. Retrieved from http://ritter.tea.state.tx.us/rules/tac/chapter113/ch113c.html.

*Chapter Three*

# A Qualitative Study of Perceptions and Experiences of Online Victim Services Academic Community Engagement

*Graduate Student Reflections*

Mary M. Breaux and James G. Booker

Given the growth in the field of victimology, more courses are not only being offered through face-to-face instruction but also through online instruction. Few studies have examined the experiences and perceptions of students who learn through the incorporation of online academic community engagement that focuses on victim services studies. Academic community engagement (ACE) is a method of teaching that combines community engagement with academic instruction, which allows students to utilize the skills and knowledge learned in the classroom to make a difference and improve life in the community by understanding their roles as community members (Sam Houston State University Community Engagement, 2016). An important factor in gaining educational outcomes in college teaching is student engagement; however, determining how to achieve greater student engagement can be complicated and complex (Perrotta & Bohan, 2013).

This study explores perceptions and experiences of graduate students who were enrolled in an online graduate victim services course and primarily work in a victim services field. A pre- and post-test survey was administered to all students who were enrolled in the course to examine their perceptions and experiences of victim service organizations in which they assist victims. Results from pre- and post-tests showed that participants learned more about their own organization and the challenges they faced while obtaining organizational information as well as resources and services for victims.

## REVIEW OF THE LITERATURE

Over the past decades, higher education has highlighted and identified community engagement as a central mission. The research and recognition behind community engagement is growing and is now viewed as a legitimate approach to producing knowledge within this area of focus (Gelmon, Jordan, & Seifer, 2013). With this in mind, the university, student, and community benefit from this type of engagement.

According to Gelmon, Jordan, and Seifer (2013), many institutions of higher education assert that they are connected to the community through their mission statement; however, only certain institutions actually reinforce this type of engagement and make it a priority for the institution. For example, Sam Houston State University (SHSU) makes it a goal to encourage students to practice and exemplify the motto, "The measure of a life is its service." Their meaning behind service is to be engaged, locally, regionally, nationally, and globally. For example, SHSU students, faculty, and staff are engaged in communities in many ways, such as civic engagement, academic community engagement, and volunteerism (Sam Houston State University Community Engagement, 2016).

The New England Resource for Higher Education defines community engagement as follows:

> Collaborations between institutions of higher education and their larger communities (local, regional/state, national, global) for the mutually beneficial exchange of knowledge and resources in a context of partnership and reciprocity. The purpose of community engagement is the partnership of college and university knowledge and resources with those of the public and private sectors to enrich scholarship, research, and creative activity; enhance curriculum, teaching and learning; prepare educated, engaged citizens; strengthen democratic values and civic responsibility; address critical societal issues; and contribute to the public good. (New England Resource Center for Higher Education, 2016)

Today, many college courses and entire degrees are offered through online instruction. Students must be engaged in order to effectively obtain a clear picture of what is to be learned in an online course. According to Perrotta and Bohan (2013), analyzing student's perception of instructional strategies is an important component of understanding which teaching methods improve engagement. Incorporating ACE requirements in courses can assist students to achieve this goal.

A study conducted by Narsavage, Batchelor, and Chen (2003) concluded that over 90% of graduate students agreed that service learning helped them understand their role as a resource to the community. ACE courses integrate community engagement into the course learning objective. This type of service learning has a positive effect on students' orientation and involvement in the community (Knapp, Fisher, & Levesque-Bristol, 2010; Markus, Howard, & King, 1993; Narsavage, Batchelor, & Chen, 2003).

Community engagement is very important within the victim services field due to the growing types of victimization in our society, which creates a need for additional community resources and services to assist victims. Additionally, graduate students enrolled in these types of courses should understand the full extent of community engagement and learn how to incorporate what they are learning in their professional victim services career and the entire community with the overall objective of assisting victims. With online education increasing, specifically in the field of criminal justice and victimology, guidance on instruction from a face-to-face format to an online format is needed to focus on potentially sensitive topics that students may have strong reactions to (Cares, Hirschel, & Williams, 2014).

Content for victim-centered courses is less suitable for traditional instructor-centered teaching such as lectures, as it relies more on building and engaging the community, which should be a model for these types of courses (Gilbert, Schiff, & Cunlife, 2013). According to Dussich (2016), the uniqueness of victimology and victim services also has a variety of needs which require different educational and teaching approaches. Additionally, "discussions of teaching victimology have led to an unparalleled body of knowledge that continues to grow and serve the needs of victims in the way we teach victimology at universities and in the way we train victim service practitioners" (Dussich, 2016, p. 493). Service learning provides students with a type of real-world experience and allows them to develop a deeper understanding of social issues and the outcome based on personal insight.

Yorio and Ye (2012) through a meta-analysis study that examined the effects of service learning on the social, personal, and cognitive outcomes of learning found that service learning had a positive effect on the understanding of social issues, personal insight, and cognitive development. According to Yorio and Ye (2012),

> Understanding of social issues can be generally conceptualized as an individual's frame of reference, which guides decision making in terms of complex social issues and includes attitudes associated with cultural awareness and tolerance of diversity; behavioral competencies, which enable students to work with individuals different from themselves; and the motivation to work toward making a difference from themselves; and the motivation to work toward making a difference in the life of the community. . . . Further, the service learning experience allows students to develop relationships with their peers and community partners within the scope of the service-learning program. (p. 12)

Establishing relationships with community partners leads to a better understanding of social justice, an ability to work with a diverse population of citizens, and a will to engage in future activities to fulfill a sense of responsibility and commitment (Morgan & Streb, 2001).

The goal of this study is to add to the body of knowledge of the academic community engagement literature by analyzing results from a pre- and post-test of victim study graduate students who work primarily for a victim services agency. The analysis will examine what students learned from the online victim service course and community collaborations, students' understanding about coordinating services to assist victims, and students' perception of responding to victim needs more effectively through service and resources.

## METHOD

### Research Participants

The researchers employed a multimethod of purposeful and convenience sampling for this study. According to Creswell, purposeful sampling allows researchers to intentionally select individuals and sites to learn or understand the central focus that hold *rich* information (Creswell, 2012). Participants consisted of graduate students enrolled in an online 6000 graduate-level criminal justice capstone course, specifically titled Coordinating Victim Services at Sam Houston State University, located in Huntsville, Texas. This course was the final course graduate students were required to complete with a grade of B or higher in order to fulfill the requirements of the Victim Services Management Master's Degree.

The course overall examined professional stakeholders in victim services delivery organizations that ensure efficient, professional, and cooperative victim-centered responses to trauma and criminal victimization. Additionally, it evaluated the preventative and reactive mechanisms available to a range of government and non-government providers and synthesized the management of these victim service provisions. Students explored the challenges of coordinating efforts between different professional organizations and ways to critically and effectively address problems. This course experience attempted to assist students in becoming a positive force in society and deepen their understanding of their role as a citizen.

The course objectives were to critically evaluate research methods for studying coordinated community response to criminal victimization, synthesize research from the literature and apply it to current issues in the field, and evaluate programs designed to address the impact of collaborative and community engagement in response to victimization. Additionally, the course was an ACE course, meaning the course set the pace for not only *learning* knowledge and skills, but also actively making a difference in the community to improve the quality of life by providing critical victim service information to agencies and organizations.

There were 26 students enrolled in the course. Of the 26 students enrolled in the course, 15 students returned both the surveys, while 8 students returned only the pre-test survey, 1 student returned only the post-test, and 2 students did not participate. Overall, there were 24 responses; however, since only 15 students returned both portions of the survey, responses from these students were examined.

Nearly all (13) of the 15 students were employed at a victim services agency. Students completed the pre-test the first week of the spring semester and completed the post-test after the course requirements were fulfilled. Each student returned the pre- and post-test to the professor via e-mail (see Textbox 3.1). The pre- and post-test surveys were developed by the researchers. Currently, there are no other valid and reliable measures associated with this tool; therefore, the results were interpreted with caution to lessen the threat to internal validity for this study.

**Textbox 3.1. Research Questions from Pre-Test and Post-Test Surveys**

With what organization are you employed?

What type of services does your organization provide to victims (if any)?

What are the top 3 agencies that you collaborate with to provide services to victims?

Do you know the mission and purpose of each agency above?

How does each organization assist victims in which you make referrals for services?

What other services do these organizations offer to victims?

Do the organizations listed above know your organizations' mission and purpose?

Are community collaborations important to you?

What are your expectations from this course?

How can agencies improve the coordination of services to assist victims?

What overall did you learn from the course?

This qualitative case study was based on Yin's (2009) framework using a qualitative case study to "retain the holistic and meaningful characteristics of real-life events" (p. 4).

Students were required to select a specific type of victimization to research and locate five community agencies that assist with this type of victimization. Students were required to gather information about each agency such as mission and purpose, details of victim services and duration of services, and their agency collaborations or partnerships. As students were informed about the services of the agencies, they were to engage and communicate these resources to other agencies who may not be familiar with the agencies' services. Students were to report in a discussion format the progress of their experience and include details of their progress, successes, challenges, and barriers after communicating with the agencies.

A content analysis was conducted to understand the student's experiences and perceptions of the online ACE course that focused on coordinating victim services. Survey questions focused on their knowledge of their employment organization, the collaborations that existed within their employment organization, the importance of community collaborations, expectations of the course, and overall knowledge gained from the course.

A coding scheme was developed to identify important topics which were organized into central themes. Topics were organized based on specific areas associated with the questions on the survey. For example, questions related to "community engagement" were categorized under "community collaborations." Topics mentioned more than twice were categorized under the major theme associated with the question. Topics were coded by the two researchers who had sufficient background knowledge in the survey subject matter. Therefore, researchers confidently interpreted the meaning of student responses.

## FINDINGS

The results from the surveys revealed that 13 out of 15 participants were employed at a victim services agency and two were unemployed (see Table 3.1).

**Table 3.1.    Pre-Test and Post-Test Results**

| Pre-Test Results | Post-Test Results |
| --- | --- |
| All participants that were employed acknowledged that they knew what type of services their agency provided with the exception of one participant. | The participants provided the same information on the post-test. |
| Four of the participants did not acknowledge any agencies in which their organization collaborates to provide services to victims, while one answer was "not applicable"; all others acknowledged | Post-test revealed that the participant that provided the "not applicable" answer in the pre-test acknowledged knowing the collaborating agencies. |

other agency collaborations that they work with daily.

| | |
|---|---|
| Less than half of the participants knew the mission and purpose of other organizations in which they collaborate. | Post-test revealed that three participants learned the mission and purpose of other organizations with which their agency collaborates daily. |
| More than half of the participants knew how each community partner organization assists victims | Post-test revealed that one student's knowledge changed of that organization to a more detailed knowledge base about community organizations. |
| Less than half of the participants responded "yes" to knowing about other services offered to victims from other organizations. Five participants responded "not applicable," while four responded "yes" to only two organizations out of three. | Post-test revealed that three participants gained knowledge about the agencies they collaborate with daily. |

Each student response underwent an item-level analysis that resulted in four major themes as shown in Textbox 3.2.

### Textbox 3.2. Students' Experiences and Perceptions of Victim-Services Academic Community Services

Central Themes
Community Collaboration Significance to Victims
Academic Community Engagement
Community Coordination Improvement Areas
Academic Engagement Areas of Learning

In what follows, the results from the participant surveys are organized around these central themes.

## Community Collaborations Significance to Victims

Overall, participants recognized more significantly the importance of community collaborations from classroom requirements. The urgency of collaborating with other agencies was "very important," "highly important," "vitally important," "extremely important," or "critically important." This realization is significant due to the fact that most of their organizations require some type of community partnerships or collaborations in order to better serve the victim population whom they serve daily.

Participants overall reported that being familiar with community collaborations could assist them in working with their own population of victims. Students indicated that many of them work with the "elderly," "veterans," "children," or "clients in general." With this acknowledgment, they could better give "support to victims," "fully help victims," and "help people who need resources." Throughout, students expressed that with collaborations, "victims have the best outcome."

When commenting on community collaborations in general, students felt that their jobs should focus on more community collaborations due to the importance in evaluating clients' services. Participants felt that a single agency could not satisfy the needs of all clients due to the overwhelming needs of specific victims, such as rape victims. Students perceived that agencies are often disconnected from other agencies as far as providing services, which often prevents victims from receiving the services they require. Participants also indicated that they felt the "need to really stay connected" with their community in order to know how to assist victims. Overall, participants made it clear that community collaborations were important.

## Academic Community Engagement Course Expectations

Participant expectations of the ACE course ranged from learning more about their own agencies to understanding how to coordinate victim services with other community agencies. Students' main expectations were to learn more about community agencies and how the roles of each agency work when coordinating services for victims. Students reported learning more about their own agencies and how they work internally and learning about other viewpoints and policies.

## Community Coordination Improvement Areas

Participants recognized throughout the duration of the course that some agencies could "better coordinate services" in order to be more effective in the community. Students also recommend that education, joint trainings, and monthly meetings were very important to effectively coordinate services for victims. Other areas students mentioned as a means of improving community collaborations were to have "better communication," "develop websites," "coordinate joint educational conferences," and "know the authority, mission and purpose of partnership agencies."

More importantly, agencies should "know about and understand people's needs." Many students found that some organizations did not have a clear understanding of the duties and responsibilities of their own internal staff. Similarly, students commented that they found that many agencies "aren't aware of the resources and services other agencies provide," thus making it difficult to coordinate victim services.

## Academic Engagement Areas of Learning

One of the main focuses of this study was to examine what graduate students learned overall from the online graduate course. The majority of students reported that they learned more about their victimization topic working with specific agencies over the semester, although they work with these organizations a great majority of their workweek. Many students were not aware of specific services offered to victims through these community agencies, that is, additional services that many agencies provide to victims. Many participants reported that when working with victims daily, there is a lack of awareness of additional services that other agencies may provide, as their goal is to obtain a specific service for the victim they are presently assisting.

Many students perceived that larger agencies have little knowledge about their own agencies and "did not realize how difficult it would be to get a response" from agencies. One student noted, "It seems as though they don't care to respond if it doesn't suit their need, which is how they often respond to victims." Participants learned that multidisciplinary teams are important for community agencies to join, specifically when working with the vast number of issues that are associated with victims of elder abuse. Additionally, students felt the need to develop social media websites to raise more awareness regarding elder abuse to provide victim-centered services.

Students reported that organizations should communicate and advocate more often to ensure that victims receive resources and services. They found that it was very challenging for them to obtain information about some organizations. The students often experienced that their information was being passed from one person to another within the organization and in some cases agencies never responded to their request to obtain additional information about victim services. One student stated, "There was a lot of disorganization and communication does get lost and seems like victims would have a hard time navigating on their own."

Some participants thought they knew the services certain organizations offered to victims; however, they quickly realized they did not know the actual services they offered to victims as they once believed. Additionally, many felt that this course assisted them in the daily responsibilities within their jobs learning more specifically about how agencies function and their policies. They indicated that the course presented a different side of victimization, showing them how to identify a productive organization and the importance of collaborations among community services.

Participants found that many agencies have similar missions, but do not work together, and as a result they felt that the system was "not necessarily created to assist victims at least not yet," but they learned how important it is for all agencies to collaborate and understand what the other does. Finally, they reported that they "learned how much more can be done for victims . . .

but it depends how committed the agency is and their budget restraints past and present."

## DISCUSSION

Colleges and universities today are more ready to incorporate academic community engagement activities within courses, specifically for victim-centered courses in which students actually either directly or indirectly interact with agencies or victims. This course focused on graduate students engaging the community through gathering information for their course requirements, while at the same time passing information on to other agencies. This study offered insight into perceptions and experiences of graduate students enrolled in an online victim services academic community engagement course and what they learned throughout its duration.

Surveys provided a better understanding of experiences and perceptions of the course and of academic community engagement in general. One major disparity in this study is that less than half of the participants knew the mission and purpose of the agencies their organizations collaborate with on a daily basis and other services those agencies provided; at the same time students echoed for community agencies to become familiar with and understand the mission and purpose of each entity while completing field requirements.

While most participants learned more detailed information about their agency during the duration of the course, it showed that participants who work within victim-centered agencies may not be knowledgeable about specific information such as victim services or resources to assist clients. Moreover, it is critical that employees of victim services agencies know more about services and resources for victims in order to effectively assist them. This is consistent with prior studies conducted in the field of professionals working in victim-centered organizations showing less knowledge about services and resources other than their own.

Vinton and Wilke (2014) conducted a study of 279 victim-centered professionals who were employed in fields such as domestic violence, victim assistance, public health, and mental health who were asked about a variety of services for victims of domestic violence. Victim-centered professionals had less knowledge about other services, specifically groups that provided special services in domestic violence shelters and the Temporary Assistance to Needy Families (TANF). Perceptions of services provided within the community varied throughout all professions such as health, law enforcement, and shelter services (Vinton & Wilke, 2014).

Overall, participants learned how challenging it can be coordinating victim-centered services in the many facets of victimization. For some students, it appeared not as difficult within their professional jobs; however from a regular citizen's perspective, many found it to be very challenging to obtain agency information and realized that it is probably a challenge for some victims to seek community services in larger cities or even rural towns.

According to Vansburger, Curtis, and Imbody (2012), professionals who work directly with elderly victims face challenges such as limited funding for training, lack of resources, and challenges working with rural populations. An area of resolve for these types of challenges is inter-professional communication, cross-training, and inter-organizational communication (Vansburger, Curtis, & Imbody, 2012; Vinton & Wilke, 2014). This is the sentiment that graduate students echoed in the responses on how to improve community collaborations coordination. Although some students felt that the course was difficult due to the level of engagement required in the course, they overall felt that it assisted them in gaining a better understanding of coordinating victim services through academic community engagement.

## LIMITATIONS

There is difficulty in generalizing results beyond the sample of graduate students due to the small number of students enrolled in the course. However, since this type of degree is only offered at the graduate level at this university, it is unlikely that it could be replicated at another university, but it could be replicated through another type of degree or major.

## CONCLUSION

Oftentimes it is challenging for institutions of higher education to engage students in the classroom, whether in face-to-face instruction or online instruction. However, preparing advanced students to become more ingrained and knowledgeable about victim services organizations requires non-traditional instruction in the classroom and more direct field experience communicating with these types of organizations. Continuing to utilize academic community engagement learning could assist students in better understanding more about services to assist victims and how to respond more effectively.

## REFERENCES

Cares, A., Hirschel, D., & Williams, L. (2014). Teaching about victimization in an online environment: Translating in person empathy and support to the Internet. *Journal of Criminal Justice Education, 25*, 405–420.
Creswell, J. (2012). *Educational research: Planning, conducting, and evaluating quantitative and qualitative research.* Boston, MA: Pearson.

Dussich, J. (2016). Teaching victimology in America: From on the job training (OJT) to PHD. *Journal of Criminal Justice Education, 25*, 486–500.

Gelmon, S., Jordan, C., & Seifer, S. (2013, July–August). Community-engaged scholarship in the academy: An action agenda." *Change*, 58–66.

Gilbert, M., Schiff, M., & Cunlife, R. (2013). Teaching restorative justice: Developing a restorative andragogy for face-to-face, online and hybrid course modalities. *Contemporary Justice Review, 16*(1), 43–69.

Knapp, T., Fisher, B., & Levesque-Bristol, C. (2010). Service-learning's impact on college students' commitment to future civic engagement, self-efficacy, and social empowerment. *Journal of Community Practice, 18*, 233–251.

Markus, G., Howard, J., & King, D. (1993). Integrating community service and classroom instruction enhances learning: Results from an experiment." *Educational Evaluation and Policy Analysis, 15*(4), 410–419.

Morgan, W., & Streb, M. (2001). Building citizenship: How student voice in service-learning develops civic values. *Social Science Quarterly, 82*, 154–170.

Narsavage, G., Batchelor, D., & Chen, Y.-J. (2003). Developing personal and community learning in graduate nursing education through community engagement. *Nursing Education Perspectives, 24*(6), 300–305.

New England Resource Center for Higher Education. (2016). Retrieved June 17, 2016 from http://www.nerche.org.

Perrotta, K. A., & Bohan, C. H. (2013). "I Hate History": A study of student engagement in community college undergraduate history courses. *Journal on Excellence in College Teaching, 24*(4), 49–75.

Sam Houston State University Community Engagement. (2016). Retrieved June 1, 2016 from https://www.shsu.edu/academics/cce.

Vansburger, E., Curtis, V., & Imbody, B. (2012). Professional preparedness to address elder abuse and neglect among elders living in rural south: Identifying resiliency where stress prevails. *Ageing International, 37*, 356–372.

Vinton, L., & Wilke, D. J. (2014). Are collaborations enough? Professionals' knowledge of victim services. *Violence against Women, 20*(6), 716–729.

Yin, R. K. (2009). *Case study research: Design and methods* (4th ed.). Los Angeles, CA: Sage.

Yorio, P. L., & Ye, F. (2012). A meta-analysis on the effects of service-learning on the social, personal, and cognitive outcomes of learning. *Academy of Management Learning & Education, 11*(1): 9–27.

*Chapter Four*

# The Impact of a Service-Learning Project Involving Pre-Service Teachers Working with Incarcerated Youth

John Kelly, Colin Dalton, and Diane M. Miller

Service learning continues to garner attention as a pedagogical strategy utilized in the training of future teachers to promote critical thinking and understanding of the culture of special populations (Hampshire, Havercroft, Luy, & Call, 2015; Mayhew & Welch, 2001). The service-learning approach enhances the standard forms of pre-service teacher (PST) fieldwork, often characterized as observations or student teaching, with elements of community service (Glazier, Able, & Charpentier, 2014). Instead of merely observing the students in traditional educational settings, service learning provides a pathway to interacting with students in diverse environments.

In this study, we analyzed the impact of a service-learning project for PSTs in a traditional teacher preparation program with an urban education focus. The service-learning project required the PSTs to participate in a literacy development project with at-risk youth detained in a juvenile detention center. We sought to assess the PSTs' attitudes and perceptions toward the culture of special populations and determine whether the service-learning project altered those attitudes and perceptions. Furthermore, this study examined the impact of the service-learning project on the PSTs' knowledge of the educational needs of at-risk youth.

## Enhancing Traditional Teacher Preparation with Service Learning

Traditionally, PSTs have engaged in fieldwork, such as student teaching, to practice the implementation of the educational theory, content-area knowledge, and teaching methods covered in their course work in preparation for teacher certification and a career in teaching. Mayhew and Welch (2001) described this traditional PST fieldwork as experiential learning primarily intended to "develop a set of professional competencies" (p. 210). This creates an atmosphere of "consumerist interaction" (p. 210) in which the PST receives knowledge and skills from an experienced teacher and practices that newfound understanding under his or her watchful eye. Such guided practice is necessary for state teacher certifications and licensure, of course, but how authentically does the traditional fieldwork engage PSTs with the diverse populations they will soon teach?

To address this question, some teacher preparation programs have sought to extend their curricula beyond the traditional models of student teaching. Service-learning projects, implemented as part of PSTs' training, seek to prepare culturally responsive teachers who will empathize with students from special populations, including racial and ethnic minorities, poor students, students with disabilities, English language learners, and at-risk, migrant, and homeless youth (National Education Agency, 2015).

For example, Davis, Emery, and Lane (1998) found that urban PSTs gained a better understanding of the high rates of poverty, at-risk factors of school failure, and poor health care services in rural communities in South Carolina through a service-learning project in which PSTs lived with mentor teachers in rural school districts. More recently, Hildenbrand and Schultz (2015) argued that PSTs need to understand that their future students bring different life experiences into the classroom, and that PSTs' empathetic approaches were fostered through community partnerships with the university teacher preparation program.

It is important to note that service learning should not be confused with community service or fieldwork. Service learning includes service to the members of the community but is complemented with an academic component that is associated more typically with fieldwork. The impact of this arrangement is both assessed and strengthened through the use of reflection. At its core, service learning is a reflective practice (McClam, Diambra, Burton, Fuss, & Fudge, 2008). These elements of community service, fieldwork, and reflection combine to produce a "distinct pedagogy" (Mayhew & Welch, 2001, p. 210).

The benefits of service learning go beyond the pedagogical knowledge acquired through traditional fieldwork. Service-learning projects can serve to broaden PSTs' perspectives on inclusivity. In their work to increase cultural responsiveness in their teacher candidates, Glazier, Able, and Charpentier (2014, p. 193) concluded that service learning provides critical benefits to PSTs since it helps to "develop civic-minded educational professionals who are committed to educating children and youth for equity and excellence."

Service learning pushes PSTs beyond the boundaries of traditional PST fieldwork. Carrington and Saggers (2008, p. 803) documented a pilot study of a service-learning program that encouraged "beginning teachers to be passionate and creative about engaging with the broader community in democratic ways, where difference and diversity are valued, and the problem of injustice and exclusion in education can be addressed and shared." These researchers concluded that service learning could act as a vehicle to challenge the traditionally hierarchal structures of education, giving rise to a more inclusive and equitable view of education.

In summary, our definition of service learning seeks to incorporate positive elements of both community service and traditional PST fieldwork including the following components:

- Introducing PSTs to special populations of students, outside of the school setting, who may enter their future classrooms.
- Introducing PSTs to the social service agencies in the community that provide services and intervene with students within special populations.
- Preparing educated, engaged PSTs with democratic values and social responsibility.
- Familiarizing PSTs with critical societal issues.
- Helping PSTs acquire knowledge and a useful understanding of the world.
- Building PSTs' critical thinking skills.
- Encouraging PSTs to contribute to the betterment of society and pass these values to their future students.

Thus, our study focused on the implementation of a service-learning project with PSTs. Since the study was conducted as a literacy project at a juvenile detention center located within the downtown court district of a major city in the southern United States, the converging concepts of service learning, special education settings, and teacher preparation served to contextualize our work.

## Service Learning at the University of Houston–Downtown

The teacher preparation program of this study is housed within a college, titled the College of Public Service, at the University of Houston–Downtown. The College of Public Service encompasses three departments—Criminal Justice, Social Work, and Urban Education—to comprehensively serve the nearby courthouses, jails, social service agencies, neighborhoods, and urban schools. Moreover, the college is organized around the belief "that, through public service, an educated society creates thoughtful policies and practices to improve the lives of diverse populations" (Van Horn, 2014, n.p.).

Since the university is located in the central business district of a metropolitan area, its programs embrace this urban location by engaging its students in a variety of profession-based, high-impact service-learning projects within the local community. In fact, service learning and community engagement are institutional priorities, and the university recently received the Community Engagement Classification from the Carnegie Foundation for the Advancement of Teaching.

## Service-Learning Projects in the Juvenile Justice System

The connection of departments—Social Work, Criminal Justice, and Urban Education—at the college level along with the university's urban location provided a natural setting for this service-learning project for PSTs at the nearby juvenile justice center. This service-learning project was specifically designed for PSTs majoring in urban education. The project was embedded within an introduction to a special populations course and represents an attempt to replicate the results of a similar service-learning project conducted with undergraduate criminal justice students working directly with incarcerated youth (Hirschinger-Blank, Simons, Finley, Clearly, & Thoerig, 2013).

In their pilot study of this service-learning project, the researchers reported that exposure to the juvenile justice system and a poverty-stricken community provided "a new lens into the complexity of the youth's daily lives," thus fostering a newfound respect for the challenges faced by the youth (p. 23). Hirschinger-Blank and colleagues found that experiencing the institutional barriers firsthand fostered a more complex understanding of delinquency. Similarly, the service-learning project for PSTs reported in this study aimed to provide a "lens" through which future teachers majoring in urban education could view the lives and educational needs of at-risk students in the juvenile detention center.

Therefore, the current study sought to assess the PSTs' attitudes and perceptions toward the culture of special populations and determine whether the service-learning project altered those attitudes and perceptions. Furthermore, this study examined the impact of the service-learning project on the PSTs' knowledge of the educational needs of at-risk youth.

## METHODS

Narrative inquiry and the resulting analysis were employed in this study because the methodology allowed for the authentic voices of the PSTs to be captured after they participated in the service-learning project at the juvenile justice center. The self-narratives written by the PSTs after participating in the service-learning project were studied and interpreted. This allowed exploration of the depth of nuanced thinking in the PSTs' attitudes and perspectives toward the incarcerated youth.

## Purpose and Research Questions

Informed by this narrative inquiry design, the authors explored the role a high-impact service-learning project had in shaping future general education teachers' attitudes toward special populations and building inclusive teaching practices in an introductory education course to special populations. The study focused on the following research questions:

1. How did the literacy project influence PSTs' attitudes and perspectives toward the culture of special populations?
2. What impact did service learning have on the PSTs' knowledge and understanding in building inclusive teaching practices?

These questions were examined within narrative documents, namely, the written reflections of the PSTs from two separate course sections. A list of guiding questions was provided to offer prompts for reflections (see Textbox 4.1).

---

**Textbox 4.1. Prompts for Reflection**
**Literacy Project: Guided Questions for the Juvenile Detention Center Experience**

1. Provide me with a one- to two-page paper (12 pt., double-spaced) using the questions as a guide; however, write your response in a narrative form that is succinct and to the point.
2. 1. Introduce yourself. Give us a quick overview of your background and where you are in your teacher prep. program. What brought you to Dr. Kelly's class, "Introduction to Special Populations"?
3. 2. Why did you choose the Harris County Juvenile Detention Center for your service-learning project (field experience)? What were your expectations?
4. 3. Describe the services you provided in the detention center, to whom, and how often. Describe anything that stood out about the student(s) whom you supported.
5. 4. Were you able to get a feel for the overall effect your work had with the youth? Did the youth implicitly or explicitly acknowledge these effects? Please describe.
6. 5. Did anything stand out or surprise you about your experience with these youth and the detention center?
7. 6. How powerful was this experience, and did it affect you personally and your teaching philosophy? Explain.

---

8. 7. Did the service-learning project provide you with a deeper understanding of the curriculum, students with disabilities, and how to support them in your classroom?
9. 8. Would you recommend this type of service-learning experience for other students, teachers, and/or professors? Why?

The reflections were written immediately after the projects were completed. Initially, each of the authors read each reflection using an open coding method to identify emerging themes and applicable segments of text. The authors then met to compare initial thematic codes to determine categorical placement in relation to the research question foci of attitudes and perspectives toward special populations and knowledge and understanding of inclusive teaching practices.

Next, the individual researchers read through the reflections a second time, performing a constant comparison of the PSTs' reflections to the newly established categories (Creswell, 2014). Finally, the authors compared their second rounds of analyses to confirm the thematic categories and reach consensus. Using an emergent coding method (Baturina, 2015; Merriam, 1998), the researchers sought to establish a triangulation of the findings across multiple transcripts.

## Participants

Participants for this qualitative interpretive study included 29 PSTs who were enrolled in face-to-face introductory courses in special education at the University of Houston–Downtown. Introduction to Special Populations, an undergraduate class for PSTs in a traditional teacher preparation program with an urban focus, introduces PSTs to exceptionalities among children with emphases on prevalence, assessment, characteristics, and classroom management. Issues of social and educational inequality in urban communities and schools are discussed, particularly those issues confronting students from low socioeconomic populations. Additionally, the course focuses on developing the conceptual knowledge of special education in pre-service general education teachers.

The participants were from two cohorts: Cohort 1 consisted of 12 PSTs (11 females and 1 male) who volunteered to participate in a literacy project in an urban juvenile detention center between January and May of 2013, and Cohort 2 consisted of 17 PSTs (14 females and 3 males) who participated in a similar literacy project between September and December of 2014. The 2013 cohort was composed of 7 Hispanic, 1 African American, and 4 Caucasian PSTs. The 2014 cohort was made up of 13 Hispanic, 2 African American, and 2 Caucasian PSTs. All met stringent requirements for entering the juvenile detention center. Each PST who participated was over 21 years of age, passed a background check, and attended an instructional tutorial given by detention staff on how to conduct themselves within the juvenile detention center.

## Juvenile Justice Center Pre-Entry Procedures

In order for the PSTs to participate in the service-learning project at the juvenile detention center, they needed to obtain security clearance from the detention center and participate in an orientation session with the community outreach coordinator at the detention center. The security clearance initially required the PSTs and participating university faculty to submit a form of state identification for an electronic background check at the county level. Once the PSTs and faculty passed this initial clearance, they submitted to fingerprinting for a national-level background check.

## Orientation to the Juvenile Justice Center

A community outreach coordinator from the juvenile detention center visited the university to provide all participants in the service-learning project with an orientation to entering the detention center, including daily operating procedures of the court and detention center and working with the students housed there. The orientation included statistical data about the juvenile justice center, the juvenile students' daily schedule, and an overview of the crimes committed by the juveniles. Most importantly, the orientation included an explanation of the social service and law enforcement agencies involved in the juvenile justice system and a description of the charter school housed within the detention center.

The community outreach coordinator also explained the legal system and how it applies to juvenile offenders. This particular juvenile detention center houses young offenders under the age of 18 waiting to attend court to face charges for a variety of major crimes. The community outreach coordinator from the juvenile justice center revealed that most youth under the age of 18 who are arrested and charged with a crime are quickly assigned a court date and released to their parents.

However, if they are charged with especially serious crimes or lack suitable parents/guardians to care for them, they must remain detained until their court dates. This is the case with the young offenders housed at this particular juvenile justice center. Interestingly, the community outreach coordinator concluded with a recruiting speech and instructions on how to apply to teach at the juvenile justice center and tutor at their summer program.

## Field Trip to the Juvenile Justice Center

Once the PSTs and university faculty completed the orientation presentation by the juvenile justice center's community outreach coordinator, they participated in a tour of the juvenile justice center. After passing through a metal detector at the entrance of the juvenile justice center, the PSTs placed all of their personal items, including cell phones, in lockers provided for guests and visiting parents. The tour included visiting the juvenile courtroom, the detention center's medical center, the gymnasium (only recently fitted with air conditioning), visiting rooms (for parents, lawyers, and social service workers to visit the detained children), and the "pods" which contain individual cells and a common area for school, meals, and downtime.

The PSTs visited on five separate mornings for three hours each visit to work with incarcerated youth. The PSTs engaged the youth with literacy-oriented activities, including original personal narrative stories, reading for enjoyment, and literary analysis tasks. The award-winning novel *The Invention of Hugo Cabret* by Brian Selznick was used as a vehicle for thinking and reflection. Although the incarcerated youth are divided homogeneously by gender, the UHD students were not paired with the youth in this way. Male and female PSTs volunteered for one of the two groups. Once they chose male or female, they stayed with the same group throughout the study.

## The School Housed Within the Juvenile Justice Center

State compulsory education laws require all children aged between 6 and 18 to attend school. Therefore, all juveniles placed in detention are provided educational services funded by the state's education agency and state and federal grants. The charter school, run by state-certified educational administrators and teachers, provides a regular school-year program, including mandated state testing and summer school, to enable detained students to continue their education.

The charter school focuses on state-mandated academic curriculum, academic remediation, vocational education, and life skills. The students remain in their pods, and state-certified content-area teachers rotate among the pods, which separate the detained youth by gender, age, and disposition. Since this service-learning project centered on literacy development, the school's principal coordinated the schedule for our pre-service teachers to visit each pod during the scheduled language arts and reading periods.

## RESULTS

The PSTs, in their written narratives, articulated their individual experiences working with the incarcerated youth on the creation of five books of personal narratives, short stories, letters, poetry, and artwork. Understandably, several participants expressed an initial trepidation prior to entering the detention center. One participant wrote about being "a little scared" upon walking into the juvenile detention center. Another participant echoed this sentiment: "When we walked through the security gates, I felt nervous about meeting these boys since I did not know how they would react to us."

However, the apprehension diminished once the interactions began. One participant noted, "Once sitting down with them and introducing ourselves, my feeling of nervousness started to fade away." Despite initial fears, all participants in this study expressed an overall satisfaction with the service-learning project at the juvenile justice center.

After transcribing and coding the PSTs' narratives using a constant-comparative method, the following three common themes emerged: awareness of at-risk youth, empathy toward at-risk youth, and the positive impact of the service-learning project on the PSTs' career choices.

## Awareness of At-Risk Youth

Several PSTs who participated in the service-learning project expressed surprise when they realized the children in the juvenile detention center were "just children," "just like me and you [sic]," "only made a mistake," and were "normal kids who made a mistake." One participant realized that the children in the detention center "have dreams and aspirations just like any other young girl would have." Another PST, while working with one of the boys in the detention center, noticed, "I was just like him." He predicted that he would "have students at risk in my future classroom."

He concluded, "Students come in all shapes and sizes; and some will come with learning disabilities, a rap sheet, and mental issues." Throughout their narratives, the PSTs revealed an increased awareness of at-risk youth. One PST reflected, "This experience has taught me that students, whether in the classroom or detention center, are still human and still want to learn."

The PSTs' preconceived notions about at-risk youth were dispelled. A participant explained, "I was expecting disinterest and a lack of cooperation from the students in the juvenile detention center, but they were more than happy to work with us and to share their unique experiences." Another PST characterized the "eye-opening" experience as "a wake-up call to be more proactive and more involved in the growth, development, and education of our youth." She "discovered that children with disabilities require more patience, love, and one-on-one time."

The PSTs learned that the children in the juvenile detention center are not inherently bad but often broke the law due to a lack of proper care and influence at home. They also noted that most of children in the detention center responded well to the individual attention provided by the service-learning project. One PST "noticed that most of them are in their situation because they have nobody at home to discipline them or care for them. Most of these kids learn everything from the streets." She inferred, "Most of these young adults are just trying to get attention from their parents and maybe even some love."

Another PST, pleasantly surprised by the detained children's demeanors, wrote, "They were all really nice and cooperative with our project, and they were excited to help other kids not get into trouble." She concluded, "This experience was a real eye-opener about troubled youth. They are not bad kids; they just have bad moments." Similarly, another participant noted, "I was surprised by how respectful they were toward me. Also by how young they all were! They seemed like babies in there."

## Empathy Toward At-Risk Youth

The data generated from the PSTs who participated in the service-learning project at the juvenile detention center reinforced positive findings generated by other studies on the impact of service-learning projects pertaining to the development of empathy toward at-risk youth (Glazier, Able, & Charpentier, 2014). Many participants in this study expressed a desire to continue helping the children in the detention center. For example, one participant wanted to continue to "give the girls hope and guidance to change." Similarly, another participant expressed a desire to "give the students hope for something better in the future rather than making the same mistakes they made in the past."

The empathetic development in PSTs was not limited to emotional compassion. Often, the PSTs' empathy toward the detailed juveniles was revealed when they expressed the desire to establish a future connection with the detained youth. They planned to act on their empathetic development. One PST stated, "I am going to try to write her while she's in the county prison." Another PST revealed her strategy to act on her empathetic development by stating, "I plan to donate children's books to the juvenile center and volunteer to read to the children."

The service-learning project also promoted empathetic awareness of the detained children's educational needs. Several narratives contained concern about the lack of materials available to the detained children during the school day. As most of the participating PSTs were familiar with modern classrooms containing smartboards, computer stations, and class-issued laptops, they logically expressed concern that the children were only permitted to use a "single pencil and one sheet of paper."

Numerous narratives presented commentary about how the juveniles were using their detention center–issued slippers as erasers. The experience allowed the PSTs to develop shared values about the need for equal educational opportunities for children across the community, including those detained for committing crimes. Many narratives included concern for the children's educational futures, a thought best expressed in one PST's proclamation, "Everyone deserves to be able to learn as much as possible, in the best way they can."

## Positive Impact of the Service-Learning Project on the Pre-Service Teachers

The PSTs who participated in the service-learning project at the juvenile justice center noted the positive impact of the project in their post-project reflections. Participants noted that it was "an honor to be a part of this exciting program," which was an "eye-opener" and a "powerful experience." One PST reflected that the experience "changed my outlook on teaching for the better."

Importantly, the experience reinforced the participants' career goals of becoming teachers and helping children. One future teacher wrote that the experience "truly inspired me and reminded me of why I chose to become a teacher" and "is a great way to remember how important our job of teaching really is." Another participant succinctly summarized the positive impact of the service-learning project on reinforcing her career goal of becoming a teacher by stating, "They have dreams and aspirations just like any other young girls would have, and that was something that truly inspired me and reminded me of why I chose to become a teacher." Many project participants noted that the service-learning project positively influenced their planned future teaching practices. One PST related, "It has been an honor to be a part of this exciting program, and hope to use what I learned in this experiment in my classroom one day."

Notably, the PSTs came to realize that the children detained in the juvenile justice center need caring teachers once the children inevitably return to their former schools. A program participant explained, "Maybe I can make a difference in at least one life by actually caring for them and their well-being, not just label them as the trouble child in the classroom." Another future teacher plans to "open [her] classroom for them as if it was their home so it can be their safe zone."

Overall, the service-learning experience reinforced course objectives related to the academic potential of at-risk students. Many PSTs in the project were pleasantly surprised with the literacy levels, artistic talent, and scholastic motivation of the students in the juvenile detention center. One participant claimed, "I feel that makes me an ambassador for the students in the juvenile center; and as the ambassador, it is my duty to share their talents and ambitions."

## Limitations

Although this research revealed key thematic findings in the area of PSTs' attitudes and perspectives toward special populations and knowledge and understanding of inclusive teaching practices, some limitations should be recognized. The data collection for this research occurred within the context of the primary author's teaching; therefore, the limitations of researcher bias and convenience sampling were inherent. To address researcher bias, second and third researchers were involved in the thematic coding and data analysis.

Each stage of analysis was strengthened by and checked for inter-coder agreement of at least 80%, a minimum percentage for qualitative reliability. Additionally, the sample of convenience limits the generalizability of the findings; however, the written reflections of the PSTs were culled from two different semesters of two separate course sections. The researchers endeavored to triangulate all findings across individually repeated readings, codings, and data sets.

## DISCUSSION

Results indicated that PSTs' attitudes, perspectives, and knowledge of the special population of incarcerated youth and their academic needs broadened as a result of the project. The PSTs' narratives illuminated components of service learning that impacted their teacher training and provided a firsthand account of their experiences working with the students detained in the juvenile justice center. Although the county's policy did not allow for post-surveys of the students that extended beyond the academic content, informal verbal feedback from the juveniles, triangulated with the administrators and the teachers, indicated that the project was positively received and exceeded expectations. The researchers concluded that all participants—the course professor, PSTs, and juvenile detention center administrators—considered the endeavor worthwhile.

It must be noted that the principal of the charter school within the juvenile detention center protected the PSTs from the more dangerous youth offenders in the detention center. Any pod the PSTs entered contained numerous guards, trained juvenile detention center teachers, and several detention center administrators. The PSTs in the service-learning project, mostly female, worked mostly with the female young offenders who were not arrested for violent crimes. Whenever potential dangers at the juvenile justice center appeared, the principal canceled the service-learning project until safe conditions prevailed.

During one semester of the implementation of the service-learning project, juvenile boys waiting trial for murder overpowered guards and escaped the detention center. Consequently, the service-learning project was postponed that semester. Unfortunately, despite the service-learning project participants' positive comments about the children in the juvenile detention center, some of the children detained at the juvenile detention center are dangerous individuals destined for life outside the law. The pre-entry training and protection provided by the charter school principal reminded the PSTs of this sad reality every time they entered the juvenile detention center.

The literacy project, funded by a community engagement grant from a state representative, allowed for the professional publication of five illustrated books containing the stories of incarcerated youths through poems, personal narratives, short stories, and artwork. Regrettably, the time delay of the professional publication of the children's work, the required anonymity of the detained children, and the transient nature of children within the juvenile justice system (both within and outside the system) prevented the children from seeing their work in published format. Also, the juvenile detention center administrators removed about 15% of the detained children's writing and artwork submissions during the editing process, deeming it to be "gang related."

Despite the complicated nature of organizing and implementing a service-learning project for PSTs in a juvenile detention center, the positive impact on the PSTs (detailed in this chapter) and the detained children (not assessed in this study) far outweighed these complications. A project participant summed up the experience, saying that she "would definitely recommend this type of service-learning experience for students, teachers, and professors. This learning experience is a great way to remember how important our job of teaching really is."

## REFERENCES

Baturina, D. (2015). In expectation of the theory: Grounded theory method. *Methodological Horizons, 10*(1), 77–90.

Carrington, S., & Saggers, B. (2008). Service learning informing the development of an inclusive ethical framework for beginning teachers. *Teaching and Teacher Education, 24*, 795–806.

Creswell, J. W. (2014). *Research design: qualitative, quantitative, and mixed methods approaches* (4th ed.). Los Angeles: Sage.

Davis, M. T., Emery, M. J., & Lane, C. (1998). Serve to learn: Making connections in rural communities." In D. Montgomery (Ed.), *Coming together: Preparing for rural special education in the 21st century.* Proceedings of the American Council on Rural Special Education, Charleston, South Carolina.

Glazier, J., Able, H., & Charpentier, A. (2014). The impact of service learning on preservice professionals' dispositions toward diversity. *Journal of Higher Education Outreach and Engagement, 18*(4), 177–198.

Hampshire, P. K., Havercroft, K., Luy, M., & Call, J. (2015). Confronting assumptions: Service learning as a medium for preparing early childhood special education preservice teachers to work with families. *Teacher Education Quarterly, 42*(1), 83–96.

Hildenbrand, S. M., & Schultz, S. M. (2015). Implementing service learning in pre-service teacher coursework. *Journal of Experiential Education, 38*(3), 262–279.

Hirschinger-Blank, N., Simons, L., Finley, L., Clearly, J., & Thoerig, M. (2013). A pilot study of a criminal justice service learning course: The value of a multicultural approach. *International Journal of Teaching and Learning in Higher Education, 25*, 14–28.

Mayhew, J., & Welch, M. (2001). A call to service: Service learning as pedagogy in special education programs. *Teacher Education and Special Education, 24*, 208–219.

McClam, T., Diambra, J. F., Burton, B., Fuss, A., & Fudge, D. L. (2008). An analysis of a service learning project: Students' expectations, concerns, and reflections. *Journal of Experiential Education, 30*, 236–249.

Merriam, S. B. (1998). *Qualitative research and case study applications in education.* San Francisco: Jossey-Bass.

National Education Agency. (2015). *Special populations backgrounder.* http://educationvotes. nea.org/wp-content/uploads/2010/05/Special-Populations-Backgrounder.pdf.

Tesch, R. (1990). *Qualitative research: Analysis types and software tools.* New York: Falmer.

Van Horn, Leigh. (2014, last modified November 2). Thinking about the mission of the college of public service. Available from http://www.uhd.edu/academic/colleges/publicservice.

*Chapter Five*

# Empowering Teachers for Linguistic Diversity

*In Search of Professional Dispositions*

## Mary A. Petrón and Baburhan Uzum

Linguistic diversity is on the rise in U.S. public schools. In Texas public schools, one out of every six children is an English language learner (ELL). The overwhelming majority are Spanish speakers from low-income families (Morgan & Vaughn, 2011). By most measures, the ELL K–12 population is not faring well in schools. According to analysis of the state's own language proficiency testing data, more than one out of every two ELL students in grades 3–12 failed to advance at least one proficiency level (*LULAC v. State of Texas*, p. 16). Their academic progress, as measured by state accountability exams, also falls significantly behind that of non-ELLs (*LULAC v. State of Texas*, p. 17).

Although the ELL population has increased significantly in Texas, the teaching workforce remains primarily monolingual and White (Ramsey, 2016). To complicate matters, English as a second language (ESL) teacher certification continues to be an add-on to general and content area certification. Teachers must simply pass an ESL certification exam; no training or course work is required by the state. Teacher preparation programs have begun to address the lack of training in the next generation of teachers. In order to effectively address the needs of linguistically diverse student populations, pre-service teachers must develop professional dispositions in which they embrace linguistic diversity, are willing to make accommodations, and foster a social justice perspective.

This chapter highlights a service-learning project in which pre-service teachers collaborated with content area teachers to create and deliver lessons that targeted learning objectives identified by content area teachers. Forty-eight pre-service teachers participated in this project at a local middle school in a high-poverty area with a history of poor academic outcomes for ELLs. The goals for this project are twofold: develop the professional dispositions of pre-service teachers and provide additional assistance to ELLs in the community.

## LITERATURE REVIEW

The development and assessment of teacher professional dispositions has been one of the most critical and contested topics in teacher education literature (Borko, Liston, & Whitcomb, 2007). In 2000, the National Council for Accreditation of Teacher Education (NCATE) adopted new standards that included professional dispositions, in addition to the necessary knowledge and skills for teacher candidates. The 2006 NCATE standards defined professional dispositions as "the values, commitments, and professional ethics that influence behaviors toward students, families, colleagues, and communities and affect student learning, motivation, and development as well as the educator's own professional growth" (p. 53).

NCATE later conceptualized professional dispositions to include the following: "All candidates are expected to demonstrate, through both verbal and nonverbal behaviors, 'classroom behaviors that are consistent with the ideas of fairness and the belief that all students can learn'" (Borko et al., 2007, p. 360). In the NCATE glossary, fairness was defined as "the commitment demonstrated in striving to meet the educational needs of all students in a caring, non-discriminatory, and equitable manner" (NCATE, 2008, p. 86).

The proponents of including professional dispositions in the NCATE standards argued that dispositions are critical for effective teaching because they are indicative of future behavior and action. Therefore, they help to address the question of whether teachers are going to apply the knowledge and skills they learned throughout their teacher education course work (Borko et al., 2007). The proponents emphasized the importance of a social justice perspective and argued that the goal of teacher education is to prepare "teachers who can teach all students well, not just those traditionally well served by schools, so that, as adults, all are able to participate equitably in the economic and political life of the country" (Villegas, 2007, p. 372).

The inclusion of professional dispositions in teacher preparation standards is not without criticism. Some have argued that teacher education programs run the risk of subscribing to a social or political agenda of indoctrination if dispositions are to be included in standards (Borko et al., 2007). Despite lack of agreement, researchers, teacher educators, and mentors continue to defend the need for developing pre-service teacher dispositions and have conducted empirical studies in various educational contexts. The common conclusion of such studies is that dispositions should be assessed and nurtured in teacher education programs (Diez, 2007; Dotger, 2010; Johnson, 2008; Johnson & Reiman, 2007; Rike & Sharp, 2008; Tangen & Beutel, 2016; Villegas, 2007).

One of the primary objectives in the literature on professional dispositions has been to formulate an uncontested definition. Johnson and Reiman (2007) suggested that it is possible to provide a theoretically sound conceptualization of dispositions, drawing from Dewey's work on understanding the moral self and neo-Kohlbergian theory (moral judgments in conjunction with other principles such as religion or culture). Johnson and Reiman defined dispositions as "attributed characteristics of a teacher that represent a trend of teacher's judgments and actions in ill-structured contexts (situations in which there is more than one way to solve a dilemma; even experts disagree on which way is the best)" (p. 677). They further argued that these dispositions develop over time as teachers engage in professional development programs, thereby lending further support to the developmental nature of dispositions (Mills & Ballantyne, 2010; Tangen & Beutal, 2016).

In order to cultivate professional dispositions, it is necessary to understand the biographical factors that influence dispositions, such as teacher identity (Day, Kington, Stobart, & Sammons, 2006), social class (Hoadley & Ensor, 2009), and teachers' race and ethnicity (Mills & Ballantyne, 2010). Any professional growth starts with self-awareness in terms of how one's own race and ethnicity, social class, and identity impact teaching and learning (Mills & Ballantyne, 2010).

In an effort to provide pre-service teachers an opportunity to reflect on their own identities and interactions with diversity, interventions or real-world simulations are commonly conducted in teacher education programs. These interventions can be in the form of auto-ethnographies that ask students to critically reflect on their own identity as teacher candidates (Mills & Ballantyne, 2010) or short field-study programs in which pre-service teachers can engage with diverse populations and navigate their existing beliefs and manage their expectations (Dotger, 2010). These experiences often serve as a catalyst, taking pre-service teachers out of their comfort zones (Tangen & Beutel, 2016), and promote emerging awareness about "how issues of race, class, gender, familial structure, dis/ability, inclusion, and religion are manifest within common classroom contexts" (Dotger, 2010, p. 809).

In order to make meaning of the intervention experiences, explicit reflection opportunities are required over the lessons learned, challenges, alignments or misalignments with current beliefs, conflicts, and dilemmas (Garmon, 2004; Johnson, 2008). In a recent study, Tangen and Beutel (2016) recommended that real-world engagement with diverse learners "assists pre-service teachers in reflecting on their possible selves as inclusive educators"

(p. 8). In addition, Johnson (2008) cautioned that without critical reflection on experiences, "students will not develop the cognitive structures necessary to make shifts in judgment schema" (p. 442).

From a developmental perspective, when pre-service teachers are afforded opportunities for self-reflection and are provided venues to engage with diverse educational contexts, they develop a social justice perspective, noticing the challenges and inequities in the learning environments of less-privileged populations (Mills & Ballantyne, 2010). A social justice outlook to teaching, even at the beginning stages, would ensure an emerging disposition to care and nurture as well as a desire to teach all students well (Villegas, 2007).

## Theoretical Framework

Academic Community Engagement (ACE) projects are also commonly known as service-learning initiatives, and the pedagogical objective is to "connect classroom content, literature, and skills to community needs" (Berger Kaye, 2010, p. 9). This study adopted the NCATE definition of service learning:

> A teaching/learning method that integrates community service into academic courses, using structured reflective thinking to enhance learning of course content. Through meaningful service, candidates are engaged in problem solving to create improved schools and communities while developing their academic skills, their sense of civic responsibility, and their understanding of social problems affecting children and families. (NCATE, 2008, p. 91)

This analysis draws from Garmon's (2004) and Mills and Ballantyne's (2010) studies on professional dispositions of pre-service teachers. Garmon conducted a qualitative case study of a 22-year-old White female teacher candidate. Analyzing the extensive interviews, the researcher identified six factors that seemed to be important in the teacher candidate's positive multicultural development. Three of these factors were dispositional and included openness to diversity, self-awareness/self-reflectiveness, and commitment to social justice. In light of these findings, he concluded that multicultural teacher education courses and field experiences are important tools to nurture multicultural awareness and sensitivity but may not be sufficient by themselves "to counteract the power of students' preexisting attitudes and beliefs" (p. 211).

In a subsequent study on multicultural awareness and sensitivity, Mills and Ballantyne (2010) proposed a hierarchical taxonomy of dispositions. Analyzing the auto-ethnographies of 48 pre-service teachers enrolled in a multicultural education course at an Australian university, the researchers found that 36 participants demonstrated self-awareness/self-reflectiveness,

19 displayed openness, and only 3 demonstrated a commitment to social justice. They argued that "these dispositions evolve developmentally: beginning with self-awareness/self-reflectiveness; moving towards openness; and finally a commitment to social justice" (p. 449). The researchers recommended that issues of social justice and diversity must be central components of all course work in teacher education programs in an effort to "develop deeper, more meaningful ways of engaging with diversity in educational settings" (p. 454).

Building on Garmon's (2004) and Mills and Ballantyne's (2010) work, this study explored how pre-service teachers developed professional dispositions through an Academic Community Engagement project that explicitly endorsed a social justice perspective. The goals of the project were as follows: (1) to promote development of the professional dispositions of pre-service teachers, and (2) to provide ELLs at a local middle school with academic support in the content areas.

## METHODS

A case study approach was used in the current study (Merriam & Tisdell, 2016) because the goal was to document how participants developed professional dispositions during an ACE project. The boundaries of the case were the two sections of an ESL methods course that participated in the Academic Community Engagement project at a local middle school.

### Research Context

Sam Houston State University (SHSU) has a long tradition of service since its inception as a normal school in 1879. It is evident in the university's motto: "The measure of a life is its service." Academic community engagement is promoted and encouraged by faculty and administrators at the college and university level.

This ACE project was conducted in collaboration with local middle school teachers. They identified topics and objectives for which ELLs needed additional language and content support.

Forty-eight pre-service teachers participated in the ACE project and study. All were White, female, monolingual English speakers. Most were studying to be elementary school teachers, although a few intended to become special education teachers. The teacher preparation program at SHSU required ESL certification for all early childhood to grade 8 teacher candidates.

Although three classes in ESL were required (multicultural education, second language acquisition, and ESL methods), there was no designated field component in any of these courses. The assumption was that the pre-service teachers would have ample opportunity to work with ELLs in their other field-based classes, but this often did not happen. While Texas is a very diverse state, these pre-service teachers had limited or no contact with ELLs in the K–12 schools they attended, nor in their university field experiences.

## Data Collection and Analysis

Semi-structured interviews (Rubin & Rubin, 2005), conducted before and after the pre-service teachers participated in the ACE project, formed the primary source of data for this study. A semi-structured interview format was chosen so that a single graduate student who was not involved in the project could conduct the interviews rather than the authors, who were seen as authority figures in the teacher preparation program. The graduate student had been trained in the principles of qualitative interviewing in a graduate research class.

Each of the two interviews per participant lasted approximately 30 minutes and was transcribed verbatim by a transcription service. Reflecting on one's own history with diversity and current actions in relation to others was an integral part of both interviews (Johnson, 2008). In the first interview, participants reflected on prior experiences with linguistic diversity in their personal and educational background. In the second, the reflections focused on their experiences working with ELLs in the ACE project.

Open, axial, and selective coding was used to analyze the interviews (Saldaña, 2013). Each of the authors studied the interview transcripts independently in order to identify preliminary categories. They shared these categories and discussed points of conflict in order to reach a consensus. The data were then coded in the same fashion to generate themes. The interviews were compared to the participants' lesson plans and post–field experience written reflections in order to triangulate the data. At every stage of data analysis, the authors coded independently before comparing coding so that they could serve as triangulating analysts (Merriam & Tisdell, 2016). Any coding discrepancies were discussed until a resolution was reached.

## RESULTS AND DISCUSSION

Reflective interviews were studied as two separate data sets (pre and post) because in the first interview they had not yet worked with ELLs; the second was conducted after the field experience. Consequently, the questions varied somewhat. Then data sets of individual students were compared. This provided the opportunity to identify general trends across participants as well as individual growth. Two major themes emerged from the data. The first involved the participants' movement from the belief that they were patient enough to work with ELLs to the willingness and necessary skills to differentiate instruction. Implicit in this movement was the shift from fear of the inability to communicate to a nuanced understanding of language proficiency.

The second theme involved nascent notions of social justice as they moved from viewing limited English proficiency as a problem of ELL motivation to one of ELLs who were ready to learn but needed appropriate instruction. In other words, ELLs were no longer seen as lazy but rather needed appropriate instruction to succeed. As Villegas (2007) has stated, "The overriding goal of a social justice agenda in teacher education is to prepare teachers who can teach all students well, not just those traditionally well served by schools" (p. 372). Throughout the ACE project, some of the participants demonstrated an awareness of systemic issues of inequity in the schooling of ELLs. In the following sections, several participants' voices are presented. These excerpts are representative examples of common responses from the majority of participants.

## Personal Characteristics to Professional Dispositions

In the pre-interviews, before the ACE project, pre-service teachers spoke of the importance of having patience when working with ELLs. Even though they had not worked with ELLs before, they believed they would be successful as ESL teachers because they were patient. For example, the way one of the pre-service teachers, Helena, commented in the pre-interview is typical of their responses when asked why they would be successful with ELLs:

> My strength would be my patience. I think I'm pretty patient. . . . Like if they are not able to get something in the lesson, I would definitely be able to just sit down with them and go over it however many times I need to go over it.

Simply being patient was sufficient to address the needs of ELLs in the classroom. If one was patient enough, ELLs would eventually "get it."

Although they believed the most important element in teaching ELLs was patience, the thought of working with ELLs was alarming to many because they had no experience with them prior to the ACE experience. In general, the pre-service teachers demonstrated some awareness of proficiency levels, speaking of true beginners as separate from those who simply lacked academic language. However, the possibility of not being able to communicate was uppermost in their minds. In another example from a pre-interview, Hadley stated,

> I'm nervous because I have never been in a situation where I've actually had to teach someone who doesn't speak English. . . . If you were to put me in a classroom with a bunch of ELLs I would just stare, I don't know what I would do. I would have no idea.

Clearly, despite all of their course work, these pre-service teachers did not feel confident in their ability to teach ELLs without practical experience doing so.

The few pre-service teachers who were not troubled by the prospect of a language barrier were those who had grown up in South Texas where they had been surrounded by both English and Spanish speakers. These individuals accepted language diversity as a fact of life. For example, Ashlynn stated, "I mean everyone was friends with everyone, it didn't matter the language. . . . No one was offended by it [referring to Spanish] . . . it was just accepted and it was comfortable."

These students understood that one's language proficiency did not dictate whether or not communication was possible. However, these students were in the minority. Instead, most feared rather than embraced language diversity. The ACE experience might afford those with limited experience with second language learners with the impetus to move them out of their comfort zone (Dotger, 2010) and face their general fear of language diversity head-on.

Despite having had course work that introduced ESL methods and currently being enrolled in an ESL methods class, the pre-service teachers made little mention of specific pedagogical tools or ESL strategies that would enable ELLs to learn the content. Some did assert that differentiated instruction would be necessary, but they provided little detail. Instead, they kept repeating that the teacher would have to accommodate as they would have to for students with exceptionalities. For example, Ashlynn stated in the pre-interview,

> I think you need to be willing to put in the time and put in the work for them, because they may take a little more time and work just like you would have to accommodate for a 504 student or a special needs student.

For the most part, they voiced the fact that accommodations and differentiated instruction were important but stopped there. Like Johnson (2008), it seemed as though they simply repeated a mantra they had memorized; however, they demonstrated little understanding of what specific strategies would be necessary in those accommodations.

In the few instances that the pre-service teacher gave specifics, the simplest and most obvious strategy for accommodations was mentioned: the need to provide visuals. In the pre-interview, Hadley stated,

> I think you would have to have like pictures. Not so much like concentrate on the words, so they get the bigger meaning across rather than being bogged down and trying to read the one sentence in it in English.

In the pre-interviews, it appeared that although they had course work in ESL methods, they could not readily use this to articulate strategies to differentiate instruction for ELLs.

It is apparent throughout the pre-interviews that the pre-service teachers believed that they possessed the personal characteristic of patience which in their minds was the most important quality needed to teach ELLs. They held the belief that ELLs could learn when teachers were willing to "put in the time and put in the work."

Certainly patience is a much-needed personal quality in the field of education (Willard-Holt, 2001). However, while patience is important, it is not enough to meet the academic and linguistic needs of ELLs. Few pre-service teachers went beyond acknowledging that some sort of accommodation was needed. They could not seem to transfer the pedagogical tools they had learned to a discussion of ways to differentiate instruction for ELLs.

However, the post-interviews told a different story. In fact, patience was not mentioned at all as a critical component of working with ELLs. Instead, specific pedagogical accommodations dominated the interviews. Another pre-service teacher, Astrid, stated in the post-interview,

> I know what to do. It is not just words on a paper. Like I know that I need to adapt instruction and I know that I need to talk slower. I know that I have to write slower. I know that I need to give more time to the students. I know that you can't rush on. So, it is the kinds of things that you have kind of taken or learned in the classroom, but now you can put into practice, so it really makes sense.

Astrid saw the value of implementing specific practices, like speaking more slowly. She did not just see the value; she demonstrated the willingness to do so. A critical component in the literature on dispositions is a willingness to adapt "lesson plans to meet the student needs and/or changing circumstances" (Rike & Sharp, 2008, p. 150).

Similar to the findings of Salazar, Lowenstein, and Brill (2010), the pre-service teachers developed a more sophisticated understanding of the diversity of language needs in a given classroom. For example, in the post-interview, Charity stated, "They were all on such different levels, like completely different ends of the spectrum. . . . Some of them I felt like knew so much more language than others. So it was just interesting that they were so like spread out." Their enhanced awareness of language proficiency levels appeared to form an integral part of the accommodations they provided in the classroom.

Through their interactions with the ELLs, the pre-service teachers began to acknowledge the complexity of teaching and learning in diverse educational contexts. This is an important step toward developing professional dispositions that embrace complexity instead of simple solutions (Salazar et al., 2010). The knowledge of the language proficiency levels translated into an awareness and willingness to differentiate according to proficiency level. For example, Sharla stated in the post-interview,

> We had one student who could speak very, very little English. So for him we had to really help him a lot, while at the other end we had students who were finishing the activity in 3 minutes and so we were like, well, how do we make it where it is on a level for this student, but also on a high level for these students. So it was very hard to fit the whole class's needs, but we had to.

As evident in this quote, pre-service teachers demonstrated the willingness to adapt instruction for all students even though it was difficult to do so.

The pre-service teachers assumed responsibility for ensuring that ELLs of vastly different proficiency levels received appropriate instruction. Without this ACE experience, they may have continued to view the educational needs of ELLs as something that could be addressed by personal characteristics such as patience rather than the professional disposition of adapting instruction to student needs.

Villegas (2007) stated that the disposition of teaching all children equitably included "the knowledge and skills needed to act accordingly" (p. 377). She acknowledged that even those individuals with a strong commitment to educating all children would not be able to meet the needs of culturally and linguistically diverse children without the experiences needed to develop the appropriate knowledge and skills.

## The Beginnings of a Social Justice Perspective

In the pre-interviews, the idea of social justice for ELLs was present only insofar as a professed commitment to language rights was concerned. This was somewhat pleasantly unexpected given the English-only attitude that is prevalent in this area. No pre-service teacher suggested that ELLs not be allowed to use their first language (L1) in the classroom. Many believed that the L1 could be used as a pedagogical support. ELLs could work together and thus provide an explanation in the L1 that they, as monolingual English-speaking teachers, could not. In addition, the pre-service teachers tended to put themselves in the shoes of ELLs and considered what it would be like to not be able to speak English. One even likened it to drowning. Thus, in terms of a social justice perspective, there were indications of humble beginnings, but a base nonetheless that could be nurtured.

In the pre-interviews, these pre-service teachers did not make connections to systemic issues that hindered the academic progress of ELLs. Instead, they saw motivation to be a critical issue. In other words, ELLs lacked sufficient motivation to take on the task of learning the language and the content. Like much of the literature on teacher candidates' beliefs about students of color, the pre-service teachers viewed ELLs to be fundamentally deficient (Hollins & Torres-Guzman, 2005).

The pre-service teachers believed they were responsible for motivating ELLs to participate because ELLs would not do so on their own. For example, in the pre-interview, Hadley stated,

> I would make sure that I didn't let that student just sit there. Sometimes maybe that student wants to sit there because it's uncomfortable for them to try to get involved because they don't speak the language. . . . So I would make sure and encourage that student to get involved with their peers and work together. I wouldn't want them to feel like they are alone.

The pre-service teachers saw themselves as cheerleaders for ELLs; they sought to "fix" what they believed to be a motivation problem.

The stereotypical binary of "normal" versus "deficient" is well documented in the field of education (Apple, 2006). In this opposition, White middle-class individuals are considered hardworking and motivated to do well in school. In contrast, minority populations, including ELLs, are seen as unmotivated and lacking a commitment to education. In the absence of direct experience with ELLs, the pre-service teachers knowingly or unknowingly relied on the dominant deficit ideology that is prevalent in the field of education (Apple, 2006).

In the post-interviews, the pre-service teachers did not mention that they needed to provide motivation to ELLs. Instead, they spoke extensively about how ready ELLs were to learn. For example, in the post-interview, Heaven stated,

> They were so involved and they were so willing to learn. . . . I mean they were just very involved in stuff. So I thought that surprised me just because I thought it was going to be very difficult for them wanting to learn.

The awareness that ELLs are already motivated is of critical importance. If a teacher believes obstacles are individual ones, like lack of motivation, it is impossible to see institutional barriers.

Like Mills and Ballantyne (2010), it was evident that the development of a social justice perspective followed an evolutionary trajectory. For many of the pre-service teachers, that evolution did not transcend the boundaries of the ESL classroom. They all praised the ESL teacher, Ms. Smith, and talked about her dedication to her ELLs and how she met their needs. However, only a few noted that this dedication to ELLs did not always extend to the general education classroom. For example, Leslie stated in the post-interview,

> In Ms. Smith's class, she kind of works with each subject so that kind of helps them. But I think they could be accommodated like in the science or the social studies classroom. In the general classroom, they could have more.

As a whole, the students believed that within the ESL classroom, appropriate accommodations were made for ELLs. However, a few expressed that general education teachers did not always meet the content and language needs of ELLs.

Only a couple of pre-service teachers went beyond the idea of making accommodations for ELLs in every class to make note of systemic injustices. For example, they called into question the distribution of resources in the school. In the post-interview, Sherry noted that the textbooks for ELLs were very outdated. She also stated, "They [ELLs] didn't have the technology that other classrooms had. It just seemed very unfair. They didn't have enough." Again, these pre-service teachers represented a very small minority, but their words were powerful. They asserted that ESL education was not a priority in terms of resources at the school.

One pre-service teacher was particularly troubled by the unfairness of standardized testing for ELLs. In the post-interview, Helena talked extensively about a boy who had only been in the country for three months. Yet the student was expected to take the state exam, STAAR, in English. She stated, "I just felt so bad like, yes, he is taking the STAAR test and he doesn't know anything and I just felt it was really bad." She later questioned why any recent arrivals would be forced to take this exam when they knew so little English. She wondered what exactly was being tested in that case.

It remains to be seen whether or not this ACE experience will translate into advocacy for ELLs. However, it is promising that a few students were able to look beyond the success or failure of their initial teaching experiences in the ESL classroom and make connections to the inequalities that ELLs faced. This is in keeping with the work of Mills and Ballantyne (2010) who found a developmental hierarchy of dispositional change where teacher candidates varied in their progress toward a commitment to social justice.

## CONCLUSION AND IMPLICATIONS

In this academic community engagement project, pre-service teachers had the opportunity to develop professional dispositions and move toward a social justice perspective through interaction with an underserved population in the community: ELLs in public schools. To this end, pre-service teachers designed and taught lessons, providing content and language support to ELLs as needed. Through their engagement with ELLs in the classroom, they moved beyond a deficit perspective of ELLs to a nascent understanding of the complexity of the diverse needs and obstacles experienced by ELLs.

However, like many short-term intervention studies, the impact was limited to what was observed during a semester. Given the developmental nature of dispositions, future studies should involve longitudinal designs.

This study highlights the value of academic community engagement as a venue for addressing community needs and providing university students with much-needed applied learning experiences. This case exemplified a collaborative partnership between a local middle school and the teacher education program. Future community engagement initiatives can seek similar collaborations in critical areas. For example, public schools across the country are struggling to provide academic resources to many underserved populations. This could include ELLs, students with exceptionalities, and those that could benefit from tutoring and/or mentoring.

## REFERENCES

Apple, M. (2006). Understanding and interrupting neoliberalism and neoconservatism in education. *Pedagogies, 1*(1), 21–26.

Berger Kaye, C. (2010). *The complete guide to service learning.* Minneapolis, MN: Free Spirit Publishing.

Borko, H., Liston, D., & Whitcomb, J. A. (2007). Apples and fishes: The debate over dispositions in teacher education. *Journal of Teacher Education, 58*(5), 359–364.

Day, C., Kington, A., Stobart, G., & Sammons, P. (2006). The personal and professional selves of teachers: Stable and unstable identities. *British Educational Research Journal, 32*(4), 601–616.

Diez, M. E. (2007). Looking back and moving forward: Three tensions in the teacher dispositions discourse. *Journal of Teacher Education, 58*(5), 388–396.

Dotger, B. H. (2010). "I had no idea": Developing dispositional awareness and sensitivity through a cross-professional pedagogy. *Teaching and Teacher Education, 26*, 805–812.

Garmon, M. A. (2004). Changing preservice teachers' attitudes/beliefs about diversity: What are the critical factors? *Journal of Teacher Education, 55*(3), 201–213.

Hoadley, U., & Ensor, P. (2009). Teachers' social class, professional dispositions, and pedagogic practice. *Teaching and Teacher Education, 25*, 876–886.

Hollins, E. R., & Torres-Guzman, M. (2005). Research on preparing teachers for diverse populations. In M. Cochran-Smith & K. Zeichner (Eds.), *Studying teacher education: The report of the AERA Panel on Research and Teacher Education* (pp. 477–544). Mahwah, NJ: Lawrence Erlbaum.

Johnson, L. E. (2008). Teacher candidate disposition: Moral judgment or regurgitation? *Journal of Moral Education, 37*(4), 429–444.

Johnson, L. E., & Reiman, A. J. (2007). Beginning teacher disposition: Examining the moral/ethical domain. *Teaching and Teacher Education, 23*(5), 676–687.

*LULAC v. State of Texas.* Civil Action No. 6:14-CV-138. (D. Texas. 2014). Retrieved from https://www.scribd.com/doc/229268862/Complaint-Filed-by-LULAC-MALDEF-against-Texas-Education-Agency-other-districts.

Merriam, S. B., & Tisdell, E. J. (2016). *Qualitative research: A guide to design and implementation.* San Francisco: Jossey-Bass.

Mills, C., & Ballantyne, J. (2010). Pre-service teachers' dispositions towards diversity: Arguing for a developmental hierarchy of change. *Teaching and Teacher Education, 26*, 447–454.

Morgan, G. P., & Vaughn, S. (2011). *A review of high school completion rates and dropout prevention for students identified with limited English proficiency: A report to the 82nd Texas legislature.* Austin: Texas Education Agency.

National Council for Accreditation of Teacher Education (NCATE). (2006). *Professional standards for the accreditation of schools, colleges, and departments of education* (2006 ed.). Washington, DC: Author.

National Council for Accreditation of Teacher Education (NCATE). (2008). *Professional standards for the accreditation of schools, colleges, and departments of education* (2008 ed.). Washington, DC: Author.

Ramsey, M. C. (2016). Employed teacher demographics 2011–2015. Retrieved from Texas Education Agency website: http://tea.texas.gov/Reports_and_Data/Educator_Data/ Educator_Reports_and_Data.

Rike, C. J., & Sharp, K. L. (2008). Assessing preservice teachers' dispositions: A critical dimension of professional preparation. *Childhood Education, 84*(3), 150–153.

Rubin, H. J., & Rubin, I. S. (2005). *Qualitative interviewing: The art of hearing data* (2nd ed.). Thousand Oaks, CA: Sage.

Salazar, M. C., Lowenstein, K. L, & Brill, A. (2010). A journey toward humanization in education. In P. Murrell, M. E. Diez, S. Feiman-Nemser, & D. L. Schussler (Eds.), *Teaching as a moral practice* (pp. 27–52). Cambridge, MA: Harvard Education Press.

Saldaña, J. (2013). *The coding manual for qualitative researchers.* London: Sage.

Stetser, M., & Stillwell, R. (2014). *Public high school four-year on-time graduation rates and event dropout rates: School years 2010–11 and 2011–12* (NCES 2014-391). Retrieved from U.S. Department of Education, National Center for Education Statistics website: http://nces. ed.gov/pubs2014/2014391.pdf.

Tangen, D., & Beutel, D. (2016). Pre-service teachers' perceptions of self as inclusive educators. *International Journal of Inclusive Education.* doi:10.1080/13603116.2016.1184327.

Villegas, A. M. (2007). Dispositions in teacher education. *Journal of Teacher Education, 58*(5), 370–380.

Willard-Holt, C. (2001). The impact of a short-term international experience for pre-service teachers. *Teaching and Teacher Education, 17*, 505–517.

*Chapter Six*

# Using a Consumer Satisfaction Survey with Clients Receiving Child-Centered Play Therapy

Denise Peterson, Yvonne Garza-Chaves, and Rick Bruhn

After a play therapy session at a public school, the four-year-old boy sat at the table and listened to his play therapist explain about how to use a thumbs-up, thumbs-horizontal, thumbs-down response to this question, "When I leave the playroom, I know I will want to come back." His response was clear and instantaneous: thumbs-up. In that moment, his play therapist, a counselor education doctoral student, had real-time feedback about how the boy valued the play therapy session.

Originally the boy's parent gave permission for the play therapy as an added counseling service to help the boy adjust to preschool. The parent and the boy also knew that the doctoral student was there because the doctoral student was also in a class, a doctoral counseling internship that required students to provide Academic Community Engagement (ACE) services. The doctoral student and her classmates were required to collect feedback on the value of the ACE service, but she knew the boy couldn't fill out a questionnaire like an adult client.

As a play therapist, the doctoral student understood that the boy could communicate through simple gestures and didn't have the language skills to understand what ACE means as a grown-up might. However, the boy did know that thumbs-up meant he agreed, and in that instant both the boy and the doctoral student had a shared sense of the value of those ACE services. With a simple gesture, this four-year-old was using non-verbal communication to complete a consumer satisfaction survey. This is a story about developing a novel, non-verbal, age-appropriate approach to rating play therapy services and about how this approach gives us another tool to communicate with children about whether or not play therapy is useful.

## COUNSELING FEEDBACK LITERATURE

Counseling session feedback benefits both the child and the counselor and is valued by mental health workers as a way to plan treatment for future sessions, as well as to assess counselor effectiveness. In the words of Claiborn and Goodyear (2005, p. 209), this feedback is "a response to an action that shapes or adjusts that action in subsequent performance." Counseling client feedback, for the young and old, is gathered for the purpose of informing and influencing future sessions.

Feedback can take many forms, including descriptions of the client's view of his or her sessions, as well as evaluations of a counselor's or other health-care worker's therapeutic demeanor during the session (Claiborn & Goodyear, 2005; Graham, Denoual, & Cairns, 2005; Shapiro, Welker, & Jacobson, 1997). When feedback is from a source perceived as sincere and reliable, it is effective in promoting positive changes with regard to the counselor-client relationship and subsequent treatment outcomes (Claiborn & Goodyear, 2005). Even when counselors are not adept at soliciting clients' views, it is still important that counselors attend to feedback about the counseling relationship (Henkelman & Paulson, 2006).

Feedback allows the client to influence and be a partner in treatment by using his or her comments about the counselor's interactions (Claiborn & Goodyear, 2005). In fact, researchers discovered that clients' views of counseling sessions are better predictors of therapeutic results than practitioners' self-evaluations of efficacy of treatment (Lambert, 2005; Lambert & Barley, 2002; Lambert & Ogles, 2004; Wampold, 2001). Other researchers offered support for the use of customer satisfaction surveys to obtain clients' perceptions of their counseling experiences by evaluating the counselor and client relationship (Carroll, 2002; Henkelman & Paulson, 2006; Lambert & Barley, 2002).

## FEEDBACK FROM CHILDREN IN PLAY THERAPY

Play therapy is a form of counseling with young children based on the premise that young children don't have the symbolic language and experience to profit from "talk therapy" (Landreth, 2002). Instead, play therapists believe that children can "work through" emotional and behavioral issues through play without having to dialogue with the adult. In child-centered play therapy treatment, progress is dependent on a strong therapeutic relationship. When children contribute their viewpoints about the play sessions, it helps play therapists reflect upon and gain understanding about how children perceive the therapeutic experience (Harcourt & Einarsdottir, 2011; Hutchfield & Coren, 2011; Messiou, 2002). Children's perspectives are essential when services are designed to promote the child's well-being (Hutchfield & Coren, 2011).

Effective, responsive child counseling service requires listening to the child's voice (Cavet & Sloper, 2004). There are several noteworthy studies supporting the value of investigating children's views on treatment. Shapiro, Welker, and Jacobson (1997) studied the responses of 150 youth, ages 11 to 17, to evaluate reliability and validity in an instrument measuring client satisfaction. They used a Likert-scale survey to address the counselor-client relationship, the benefits of counseling, and the counseling process.

Shapiro et al. (1997) reported that questions such as "Do you feel better because you went, or did counseling make you feel worse, or do you feel about the same as you did before counseling?" (p. 90) were readily understood by the participants and provided information useful for enhancing counseling services. Additionally they concluded that consumer satisfaction surveys have value in treatment evaluation because the surveys can explore the client's experience of the therapeutic process and relationship. In another study with 120 children, ages 6 to 18, Van Laerhoven, Van Der Zaag-Loonen, and Derkx (2004) concluded that children preferred the use of Likert-style scales over simple numeric and visual analogue scales.

Jo Carroll (2002) wanted to give her play therapy clients the opportunity to express their opinions regarding their counseling experience because she saw this as a means to improve her clinical skills across sessions. Using a qualitative methodology, Carroll explored in detail the experiences of 14 children between the ages of 9 and 14 who had positive experiences in therapy. She found that the children's opinions encouraged the therapist's deeper reflection about her practice.

Carroll concluded that when a therapist asks a client about the therapy experience, the child can offer value-added information about her or his experience. Secondly, Carroll supported the idea that play therapists need to collect information from their clients, even if young children can't read a questionnaire. Although her research focused on a small number of children, Carroll offered support regarding the value of children's feedback forms with play therapy clients.

When reflecting on play therapy sessions, it is possible to notice that the child's verbal and non-verbal communication has a formative impact on the play therapist's performance. While Carroll supported the notion of asking for feedback in play therapy there were no other professional articles describing how to conduct a post-session survey from pre-school-age children. It was expedient to develop and field-test our own customer satisfaction survey for getting feedback from child clients receiving child-centered play therapy.

Even while pondering how to create a developmentally appropriate survey, we considered the ethical and social justice components to seeking feedback from counseling clients. The Code of Ethics of the American Counseling Association (2005) includes an expectation that counselors regularly review the therapeutic process with their clients for the purpose of evaluating the child's experience of the session. This mirrors the global politic of the 1983 United Nations Convention on the Rights of the Child, which advocated that children have the right to be heard and that their feelings and opinions need to be considered (Taylor, 2000).

## CREATING THE SURVEY

Our doctoral counseling intern and play therapist, Denise Peterson, started with a Likert-style survey called the Academic Civic Engagement (ACE) Survey, created for use with youth and adults. The initial ACE survey questionnaire was developed in order to meet the counselor internship course requirement in which doctoral students solicited client feedback for the client-perceived value of Academic Community Engagement service. Specifically, counseling students asked for client feedback using a consumer satisfaction survey intended for older youth and adults with established reading skills. Thinking about the developmental level of the four- and five-year-olds, Peterson wondered how to make a survey that didn't require high-level symbolic language.

Developmentally, by age four, children understand that symbols have a representational function and can be used in social reference. Since no studies were found that used pictorial-style Likert scales with children, the authors developed a unique system of symbols, graphics, and pictures as a way of communicating with young children to gather feedback about effectiveness and satisfaction. This led to the use of the graphics of thumbs-up, thumbs-down, and thumbs-horizontal to present the Likert-style scale choices to clients. Peterson named the scale the Play Therapy Consumer Satisfaction Survey (PTCSS) with the hope that the PTCSS offers a format for play therapy client(s) to communicate a child's perception of the session in a way that is developmentally appropriate (Henkelman & Paulson, 2006).

The PTCSS is a questionnaire that uses a visual and kinesthetic style of response in order to better meet the developmental level of the young child client. The ACE feedback survey was adapted for use with pre-kindergarten play therapy clients between the ages of four and five, resulting in the PTCSS.

Initially Peterson created a client response survey in which the questions were in the form of a Likert-style rating scale from 1 to 5, with one being "low" and 5 being "high" or "greatest value." Soon, however, adjustments were made in the belief that a visual and kinesthetic image format might increase the child's understanding of the question and therefore the accuracy of the child's responses. The Likert-type scale using pictorial images of thumbs-up, thumbs-horizontal, and thumbs-down, illustrated in Figure 6.1, was used to replace the numbered scale of the original ACE survey. Thumbs-down denoted a variety of negative responses including "no," or "not at all." Thumbs-up represented positive responses such as "yes," "most of the time," and "all the time." The thumbs-horizontal image signified "not so much" or "somewhat" and indicated that the child expressed some displeasure although the experience was not completely negative.

Before using the PTCSS, the play therapist trained children in the meaning of the hand signs. The child was asked to think about chocolate milk, and then the play therapist demonstrated that thumbs-up indicated "I like chocolate milk a lot," thumbs-horizontal indicated "a little," and thumbs-down indicated "not at all." It took approximately 5 minutes in a single demonstration for the children to learn to use the response choice. Then the PTCSS was used at the end of each session.

During development of the PTCSS, consideration was given to the implied message to the young play therapy clients that the therapist values the client's perspective regarding the therapist-client relationship. Other implied messages are that the play therapy client is capable, respected, and accepted. Even though clients are reluctant to discuss negative aspects of the counseling experience, it is also wise to gather information in a manner that is less threatening to the client.

## PTCSS QUESTIONS

In order to make a child-friendly survey, the original questions of the adult version of the ACE consumer satisfaction survey were altered to align with the developmental and cognitive needs of the pre-kindergarten child. Children are less sophisticated than adults in verbal expression, abstract reasoning, and cognitive abilities. However, it is possible for the children to express

**Figure 6.1.   Response Choices for the PTCSS**

*ACE Play Therapy Customer Satisfaction Survey*
*Service by Sam Houston State University Counseling Intern*
*Academic Community Engagement (ACE)*

*I am in school like you and my teachers want to know how I'm doing. I would appreciate your help in letting them know about me by answering a few questions about our play sessions. Choose the "thumb" that shows how you feel about the following statements.*

*The SHSU Play Friend provided special play time to me for:*

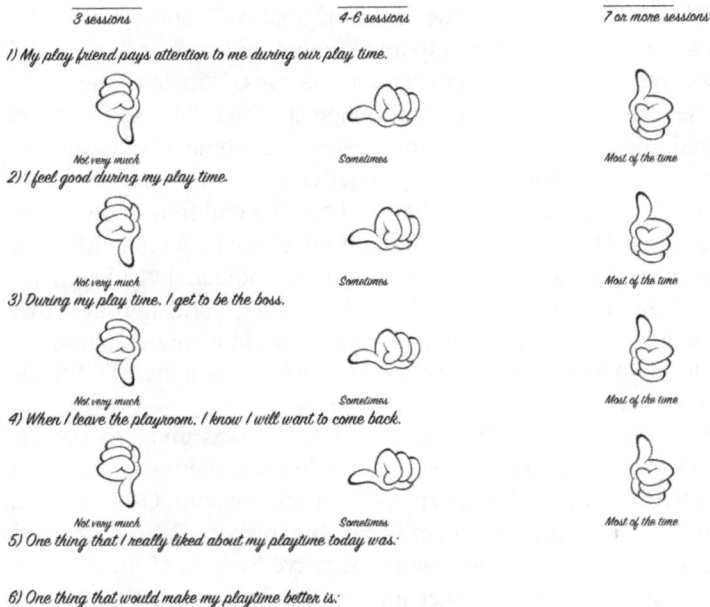

| 3 sessions | 4-6 sessions | 7 or more sessions |
|---|---|---|

*1) My play friend pays attention to me during our play time.*

Not very much           Sometimes           Most of the time

*2) I feel good during my play time.*

Not very much           Sometimes           Most of the time

*3) During my play time, I get to be the boss.*

Not very much           Sometimes           Most of the time

*4) When I leave the playroom, I know I will want to come back.*

Not very much           Sometimes           Most of the time

*5) One thing that I really liked about my playtime today was:*

*6) One thing that would make my playtime better is:*

**Figure 6.2. The Play Therapy Consumer Service Scale**

their thoughts, feelings, and experiences in a developmentally appropriate fashion (Landreth, Homeyer, & Morrison, 2006; Watts & Garza, 2008).

Table 6.1 presents a crosswalk of the statements from both the original ACE consumer satisfaction survey (left column) and the PTCSS questions (right column).

As the counseling internship semester progressed, we noticed that the children appeared to enjoy this post-session process regardless of whether the feedback was positive or included negative or contradictory feelings. On occasion children inquired about the survey as if to ensure that they had their time to voice their opinion.

As the PTCSS originated from a course assignment, the play therapist introduced the survey this way: "I am in school like you, and my teachers want to know how I'm doing. I would appreciate your help in letting me

**Table 6.1. Comparison of Customer Service Questions**

| ACE Items | PTCSS Items |
| --- | --- |
| 1) I have felt deeply understood by the Counseling Intern. | 1) My play friend pays attention to me during our play time. |
| 2) I have felt respected by the Counseling Intern. | 2) I feel good during my play time. |
| | 3) During my playtime, I get to be the boss. |
| 3) The Counseling Intern worked to help me improve the quality of my life. | 4) When I leave the playroom, I want to come back. |
| 4) Please comment on how the service provided by the Counseling Intern has helped to improve the quality of your life. | 5) One thing I really liked about my playtime today was: |
| | 6) One thing that would make my playtime better is: |

know by answering a few questions about our playtime together. Choose the thumb that best shows how you feel about the following statement."

The play therapist repeated the directions to meet the individual needs of the child clients when necessary. After the directions were given, the statements were read, and when needed the play therapist modeled the thumb responses to elicit a physical gesture from the client. In a few instances, the therapy session was a group of two children, and the therapist's initial directions included a tone inflection to indicate that the survey was about the therapist, not the other child in the group.

## The Sample

Approximately 20 child clients receiving play therapy participated. The children were in a university-sponsored play therapy center at a public preschool. All clients were teacher referred. Two-thirds of the clients served were male. Four clients in the sample had been abused and were referred because of consequent emotional and behavioral difficulties. Other clients in this sample presented with anxiety or aggressive tendencies resulting in class disruption that hindered their ability to learn.

## My Play Friend Pays Attention to Me

The first question from the original ACE survey was, "I have felt deeply understood by the counseling intern," which was adjusted in the PTCSS to state, "My play friend pays attention to me during our playtime." The statement's purpose was to assess the play therapy client's perception of the play therapist's ability to validate the client's experience. Much like the adult question, this statement evaluates the child client's perception of the play therapist's caring and empathy toward the client. Empathic responses are used to let the children know they are heard, understood, accepted, and valued as well as to enhance the child-counselor relationship (Garza & Bruhn, 2011; Landreth, 2002).

The clients' response to the statement is also a measure of his or her perception of the play therapist's ability to be present with and accepting of that child, consequently allowing the child the freedom to accept herself or himself while facilitating trust in the counselor (Landreth, 2002). The question also addressed the importance of the willingness of the play therapist, as perceived by the child, to appreciate the child as an individual. A thumbs-up response indicates that for this session the child perceived the counselor as successfully conveying the message that the play therapist is here with the child, understands the child, and cares about the child.

Children appeared to understand the question, and in most cases the authors found that most children selected thumbs-up for most of the play sessions. However, in one instance a child selected thumbs-down after an intense group (two children) play therapy session. After exploring one boy's response, the authors learned that his negative gesture was directed toward his group partner, who ignored repeated requests to be less aggressive during the session, rather than toward the therapist. His response highlighted another opportunity for use of the PTCSS, and it was subsequently used, outside of the ACE class, to solicit feedback regarding group play therapy members' appraisal of their interaction with each other after a group session.

## I Get to Be the Boss

The ACE statement "I have felt respected by the Counseling Intern" went through two revisions. The purpose of this question on the PTCSS was to investigate the children's perceptions concerning their opportunities to lead the session. In child-centered play therapy, the child is given the lead in the belief that the child is striving for inner balance and has the capacity to make choices that are growth enhancing (Landreth, 2002). The statement, "During my playtime, I get to be the boss," implies to the child that the play therapist accepts the child as an individual and is willing to follow the child's lead.

The play therapist is also trying to convey that the play therapist values the child's opinion. Further, asking the child's opinion supports the notion that the child has the capacity to rely on his or her own inner resources to self-regulate. For some children it is necessary to set numerous limits in order to protect the child, the play therapist, and the place space. These limits may affect a child's response.

When first attempted with group play therapy participants, the authors began by using "During my playtime, me and my play friend are in charge." However, this appeared to cause confusion as evidenced by children's perplexed looks and subsequent play therapist attempts to clarify the statement. One group play therapy client required substantial limit setting during sessions to protect the playroom, the safety of the other child, and the aggressive client's safety. When asked to complete the form, the aggressive child consistently responded to the question with a thumbs-down response. After some discussion, we felt that setting limits may be incongruent with the concept of "being in charge." The PTCSS statement was refined to "During my playtime, I get to be the boss." Children were directed to select either thumbs-up to indicate that they perceived themselves as in charge, thumbs-horizontal for some of the time, or thumbs-down for not at all.

## I Feel Good and I Want to Come Back

To elicit the children's opinions with regard to the value of the play experience, we developed the questions "I feel good during my playtime" and "When I leave the playroom, I want to come back." The original ACE question, "The Counseling Intern worked to help me improve my quality of life," required sophisticated abstract thinking involving contemplation of a combined set of previous experiences before producing an evaluation, which most pre-kindergarten children cannot do.

The response to "I feel good during my playtime" usually resulted in a thumps-up. While the word "play" implies fun, we realized that play therapy often involves expression of unresolved feelings, catharsis of unresolved trauma, setting of limits, and the child's dissatisfaction with the limits which have been set. We noticed that some children selected the thumbs-horizontal or thumbs-down when the play therapy involved emotionally laden play.

For example, one client selected the thumbs-horizontal response after a session in which he hid under a table and behind a curtain. He had received consequences for behavioral concerns in the classroom before the session, and as he continued in this vein, his behavior required the play therapist to set numerous limits in the playroom. Another child used the thumbs-down to express his displeasure with his group play partner's rough treatment in the playroom and the group partner's dominance over the toys and space in playroom. His play friend bumped him with the bop bag, hit him in the face with a ball, and tried to cut his shirt with scissors.

When questioned about his thumb-down response, the mistreated boy said that he did not like it when his play friend was mean to him. Using the thumbs-down conveyed, in the child's own language, that he did not feel safe. He stated the he did not like it when his group partner hurt him and did not let him play. Since the form was completed immediately following the session, it served multiple purposes, including providing an opportunity for the client to verbalize his feelings, allowing his group partner to receive information regarding his behavior from another's perspective, and encouraging the play therapist to make reflections related to the interrelationship challenges.

The play therapist did use reflection to validate the non-aggressive boy's feedback and to offer the aggressive boy the opportunity to "hear" the immediate feedback. Over time the play therapist noted changes in the aggressive boy's behavior, an indication that the feedback was "heard." Another child participating in group play therapy sessions selected the thumbs-down to reflect his displeasure with regard to his group partner's aggressive behavior.

The statement "When I leave the playroom, I want to come back" received thumbs-up from all children participating in play therapy, with one notable exception. This child's play displayed predominant themes of power and control which required frequent limit setting. During the session, the child engaged in a water and sand activity that was restricted to a vinyl tablecloth. After several reminders that the sand, water, and mud needed to stay on the tablecloth, the ultimate limit was set and the material was removed. Through the PTSCC, the child expressed her displeasure by responding to the question about coming back to the playroom with a thumbs-down.

## Likes and Improvements

The ACE form's "Please comment on how the service provided by the Counseling Intern has helped to improve the quality of your life" was deemed too complex for young children. Therefore, age-appropriate modifications were made using two questions. The first statement, "One thing I really liked about my playtime today was:" can be directed toward identifying the client's positive experience in the playroom. Children's responses reflected their enjoyment in being allowed to play freely and included comments such as "We all played," "Playing and drawing," and "Digging in the sand."

The second question, "One thing that would make my playtime better is:" was designed to investigate negative aspects of the child's play therapy experience. When developing the questions, the authors assumed that the question would be a stimulus for children to express unmet needs with regard to activities and toys. However, the responses seemed to reflect the children's positive experiences of the session. One child commented that playtime could be improved by allowing for "more time," and another responded that playtime could be improved by his "coming back."

Soliciting feedback from clients is not without its challenges (Henkelman & Paulson, 2006). The child who required numerous limits when mixing sand and water responded to the survey questions with a thumb-down. Although negative responses may be unpleasant for the play therapist, allowing the children to express an evaluation of the play session, even when angry, implies that the play therapist accepts the child as an individual and values the child's opinion of the shared experience. In addition, it demonstrates that the play therapist is willing to allow the child to be a partner in the play experience.

## DISCUSSION

The PTCSS can be used to obtain the client's perception of the play therapy experience, including the therapeutic relationship between play therapist and child. Additionally, the PTCSS can be used to gather feedback on the child's experiences with services offered through an Academic Community Engagement program. As a tool for play therapists, this scale has the pragmatic value of serving as a vehicle for the play therapist to reflect on the child's experience and to reflect on the play therapist's experiences within the session.

The feedback and reflection process can also serve as a bridge for experienced play therapists to connect the events and meanings from one play therapy session to another. For example, the boy who signaled thumbs-horizontal to give feedback to the aggressive play partner stimulated a reflection in the play therapist. She wondered what she might do or say in a future play session to create an environment where the aggressive boy can explore other behaviors, including non-aggressive, age-appropriate play with his play partner.

A feedback tool like the PTCSS can aid a play therapist in deriving new insights into the child's emotional experience in the play session or into new social, psychological, or developmental issues the child might be working through. At other times the PTCSS will help the play therapist to think about his or her own actions and role, including limit setting or considering options for reflecting play themes. Sometimes the reflective process helps the play therapist think about ways to reflect new and deeper developmentally appropriate meanings to the child to support the child's development in social, psychological, and behavioral areas (Garza & Bruhn, 2011).

Client feedback is a valuable component of measuring treatment efficacy and can assist play therapists to reflect on their techniques and effectiveness. Although the reason for creating the PTCSS was to acquire "community member" feedback for the Academic Civic Engagement (ACE) component that was required in a graduate class, the greater value of the PTCSS is to intentionally make a place for the child's feedback about play therapy services rendered. This was a small-size, qualitative, exploratory project, so readers should use the PTCSS with caution and limit use to four- and five-year-old children.

Children younger than three years old lack meta-representational under-standing of beliefs that help with understanding symbols (Callaghan, Rochat, & Corbit, 2012). We have no evidence that this scale will be of use with younger children, and we think the younger child may not be able to fully respond to the concepts and language used in the PTCSS. However, the PTCSS holds promise as an avenue for inviting and gathering play therapy client feedback in a way that demonstrates that children are valued as people and worthy of respect (Landreth, 2002). There is value in making the effort to listen to the community member's (child's) perspective. As adults receiving feedback from children about play therapy and Academic Community Engagement, we feel humble and honored.

## REFERENCES

American Counseling Association. (2005). *ACA code of ethics*. Alexandria, VA: Author.
Callaghan, T. C., Rochat, P., & Corbit, J. (2012). Young children's knowledge of the represen-tational function of pictorial symbols: Development, across preschool years in three cul-tures. *Journal of Cognition and Development, 13*(3), 320–353. doi:10.1080/15248372.2011.587853.
Carroll, J. (2002). Play therapy: The children's views. *Child and Family Social Work, 7*(3), 177–187. doi:10:1146/j.1365-2206.2002.00234.x.
Cavet, J., & Sloper, P. (2004). The participation of children and young people in decisions about UK service development. *Child: Care, Health, and Development, 30*(6), 631–621. doi:10:1111/j.1365-2214.2004.00470.x.
Claiborn, CC. D., & Goodyear, R. K. (2005). Feedback in psychotherapy. *Journal of Clinical Psychology: In Session, 61*(2), 209–217. doi:10.1002/jclp.20112.
Garza, Y., & Bruhn, R. A. (2011). Empathy in play therapy: A case analysis through two theoretical perspectives. In Danielle J. Scapaletti (Ed.), *Psychology of empathy* (pp. 167–184). New York: Nova Science Publishers.
Graham, J., Denoual, I., & Cairns, D. (2005). Happy with your care? *Journal of Psychiatric and Mental Health Nursing, 12*(2), 173–178. doi:10.1111/j.1365-2850.2004.00814.x.
Harcourt, D., & Einarsdottir, J. (2011). Introducing children's perspectives and participation in research. *European Early Childhood Education Research Journal, 19*, 301–307. doi:10.1080/1350293X.2011.597962.
Henkelman, J., & Paulson, B. (2006). The client as expert: Researching hindering experiences in counseling. *Counseling Psychology Quarterly, 19*, 139–150. doi:10.1080/09515070600788303.
Hutchfield, J., & Coren, E. (2011). The child's voice in service evaluation: Ethical and method-ological issues. *Child Abuse Review, 20*(3), 173–186. doi:10.1002/car.1142.
Lambert, M. J. (2005). Emerging methods for providing clinicians with timely feedback on treatment effectiveness: An introduction. *Journal of Clinical Psychology: In Session, 61*(2), 141–144. doi:10.1002/jcpl20106.
Lambert, M. J., & Barley, D. E. (2002). Research summary on the therapeutic relationship and psychotherapy outcome. In John C. Norcross (Ed.), *Psychotherapy relationships that work: Counselor contributions and responsiveness to patients* (pp. 17–32). New York: Oxford University Press.
Lambert, M. J., & Ogles, B. M. (2004). The efficacy and effectiveness of psychotherapy. In Michael J. Lambert (Ed.), *Bergin and Garfield's handbook of psychotherapy and behavior change* (5th ed., pp. 139–193). New York: Wiley.
Landreth, G. (2002). *Play therapy: The art of the relationship* (2nd ed.). New York: Brunner Routledge.

Landreth, G., Homeyer, L., & Morrison, M. (2006). Play as the language of children's feelings. In Doris Fromberg & Doris Bergen (Ed.), *Play from birth to twelve: Contexts, perspectives, and meaning* (2nd ed., pp. 47–52). New York: Routledge.

Messiou, K. (2002). Marginalisation in primary schools: Listening to children's voices. *Support for Learning, 17*(3), 117–121. doi:10.1111/1467-9604.00249.

Shapiro, J. P., Welker, C. J., & Jacobson, B. J. (1997). The youth client satisfaction questionnaire: Development, construct validation, and factor structure. *Journal of Child Clinical Psychology, 26*(1), 87–98.

Taylor, A. (2000). The UN convention on the rights of the child: Giving children a voice. In Ann Lewis & Geoff Lindsay (Eds.), *Researching children's perspective* (pp. 210–233). Buckingham, England: Open University Press.

Van Laerhoven, H., Van Der Zaag-Loonen, H. J., & Derkx, B. H. F. (2004). A comparison of Likert scale and visual analogue scales as response options in children's questionnaires. *Acta Paediatrica, 93*(6), 830–835. doi:10.1080/08035250410026572.

Wampold, B. E. (2001). *The great psychotherapy debate: Models, methods, and findings.* Mahwah, NJ: Lawrence Erlbaum Associates.

Watts, R. E., & Garza, Y. (2008). A constructivist approach to child-centered play therapy. In Jonathan D. Raskin & Sara K. Bridges (Eds.), *Studies in Meaning 3: Constructivist Psychology in the Real World* (pp. 145–164). New York: Pace University Press.

*Chapter Seven*

# International Service Learning

*Experiences of Mainstream Pre-Service Teachers*
*Teaching EFL in Naples, Italy*

## Burcu Ates and Yurimi Grigsby

Study abroad and international service learning (ISL) are two suggested experiences that prepare students to be active, global citizens in the 21st century (Bringle & Hatcher, 2011; Larsen, 2014). While study abroad is a familiar concept, international service learning (ISL) may not be. The ISL literature is fairly recent (Bamber, 2015); however, as noted in the following description, ISL has its roots in service learning, study abroad, international education, experiential learning, and cross-cultural communication (Bringle & Hatcher, 2011; Crabtree, 2008).

ISL is a pedagogical activity that blends academic instruction and student learning with community-based service in an international setting (Bamber, 2016; Crabtree, 2008). As Bamber (2016) argues, ISL can be described as an ecological connection with moral and even spiritual dimensions that are realized through participating in the lives and interacting with the "worlds" of others outside of one's familiar country. Bamber further explains that the experience should not only facilitate an opportunity for reflection that increases one's sense of one's own efficacy but should produce citizenry who create a more livable society.

Community-based programs and experiential learning activities for students in international settings can enhance global understanding and citizenship, awareness on empathy, and professional identity (Crabtree, 2008; Craigen & Sparkman, 2014). Meaningful community service activities incorporate educational objectives of the course and community partners' identified needs where the activities practiced and implemented are valuable to both students and the host community (Bringle & Hatcher, 2011).

Study abroad and ISL could lead to transformative learning (Vatalaro, Szente, & Levin, 2015). Transformative learning can help develop the "authentic self: ongoing process of becoming oneself" (Bamber, 2016, p. 7) and has characteristics which are "cognitive (concerned with thinking), emotional, affective (concerned with values and feelings), conative (concerned with striving, action and doing) and relational" (Bamber, 2016, p. 16). ISL contributes to social change through transforming the attitudes, values, and beliefs of participating students (Bringle & Hatcher, 2011).

This chapter specifically examines how an ISL experience facilitated three mainstream pre-service teachers in forming their professional identity as well as how it helped support their intercultural competence. Intercultural competence, an important skill today, will be a critical component in the next decade as the student population worldwide increases in diversity.

## LITERATURE REVIEW

### Teacher Preparation and ISL

The U.S. population is growing increasingly more diverse (Frey, 2015). The classroom is a mirror to the community outside its walls, which means teachers will encounter students with more diverse religions, cultural practices, and languages than in previous generations. Being involved in ISL is especially important for future teacher candidates.

According to the National Forum on Education Statistics (2016), White students enrolled in public schools decreased from 59% to 50% between fall 2003 and 2013, while enrollments of Hispanic students increased from 19% to 25%. The number of White students enrolled in public schools is projected to decrease between fall 2014 and 2025. Even though the nation's students continue to increase in diversity, the education workforce's diversity makeup has not kept pace (Schmitz, Nourse, & Ross, 2013). The teaching force in pre-K–12 classrooms in the United States is predominantly White, female, monolingual native English speaker, and middle class (Neal, Sleeter, & Kumashiro, 2015). This mismatch between mainstream teachers and students is a concern for teacher preparation programs and teacher educators. But who are the mainstream teachers? They are defined as content area teachers in English language arts, social studies, mathematics, and science (Pettit, 2011).

One of the responsibilities of teacher educators is to prepare and equip pre-service teachers with knowledge, skills, and dispositions to address and meet the needs of racially, ethnically, culturally, and linguistically diverse students. In preparation for working with culturally and linguistically diverse students specifically, some of the recommendations for mainstream pre-service teachers are the need for developing knowledge of language learning and linguistics, studying a second language, and being involved in various field experiences internationally (e.g., study abroad, ISL, and international teaching practicum) (Fitts & Gross, 2012).

Limited literature exists that highlights the experiences of pre-service teachers in study abroad programs (e.g., Petrón & Ates, 2015; Rodríguez, 2011). However, an even smaller number of studies focuses on the experiences of pre-service teachers who have been directly involved in international field experiences (e.g., Sharma, Rahatzad, & Phillion, 2013). Miller and Gonzalez's (2010) critical study, for example, examined pre-service teacher outcomes linked with service learning in domestic settings (Orange County, California) and international settings (Shanghai and Changshu, China). Both domestic and international service-learning participants reported that these experiences supported academic achievement and opportunities for career goal clarification, as well as their abilities to apply course content. However, international service-learning participants reported greater benefits in terms of understanding challenges and resources within the placement site/community. They also reported higher gains in the "use of more diverse strategies to facilitate communication with and understanding for the children with whom they interacted" (p. 34).

The pre- and in-service teachers who went abroad in this study applied the practical skills they were learning in their teacher education programs as they taught English as a foreign language (EFL). This opportunity was available to them as part of their service-learning experience. Even though the results were positive, there are still a small number of studies that exist in the literature of the teaching English to speakers of other languages (TESOL) field that discuss similar ISL setup and experiences. We believe this study will add evidence for creating similar experiences within other teacher education programs.

## Communities of Practice

Teachers must be knowledgeable about the classrooms in which they teach. This means they are competent in meeting the rigorous demands of their profession as well as familiar with the students—their abilities, their personalities, and how to engage them. In essence, teachers must turn their classrooms into communities, safe places where mistakes can be made and learning is supported in myriad ways.

New teachers may have difficulty in knowing how to create or seeing the value of creating a learning community for their students if they have not participated in such an experience while they were students themselves, for good reason. Teaching and learning are largely hands-on, social events. Researchers have long described communities of practice as a model and framework for connecting *knowing* and *doing* (Buysse, Sparkman, & Wesley, 2013; Lave & Wegner, 1991).

Additionally, communities of practice are used for continuing to meet professional learning needs (Green, Hibbins, Houghton, & Ruutz, 2013) during the first critical years of teaching, through interaction with peers in ways that foster learning and information sharing (Li et al., 2009). For example, Nistor et al. (2015) studied group cohesion and found that a sense of community (SOC) was a significantly important ingredient for building a community and motivation for knowledge sharing, as well as knowledge acceptance within the group.

Service learning allows pre-service teachers to become members of a community of practice and enhance their understanding of teaching practice, who they are and what they know. Through such active participation, pre-service teachers are exposed to multiple opportunities to collaborate and make meaning of their engagement and hopefully understand the struggles of non-native English-speaking students in their future teachings.

## Teacher Professional Identity

With unrelenting pressure for teachers to "teach to the test" on high-stakes standardized achievement tests, the professional identity of teachers has undergone a huge shift in recent years. The work and role of teachers must mean more than giving tests and being scrutinized with greater demands for accountability (Danielson, 2016). As Haddix (2015) explains, teachers must also undergo "critical interrogation of their social locations and the ways they engage with the realities of teaching and learning" (p. 63) by interacting with their communities and the culture(s) present.

As TESOL educators, this means teachers are getting to know their communities at the same time as they are getting to know themselves as teachers of their content, teachers of their particular mix of students, and teachers of the English language. Teachers are learning the profession while (sometimes) discovering what they still believe and value. Further, falling within sociocultural concerns, as a higher percentage of the teaching force is young and female, many teachers might also be juggling the responsibilities and cultural expectations.

Although teacher professional identity is not a new research area (emerging in the mid-1990s as a separate research focus), how it occurs can still be rather muddy and complex. The process of becoming a professional is called professional socialization (Brody, Vissa, & Weathers, 2010). As Brody, Vissa, and Weathers (2010) explain, professional socialization is "the process of developing a role-based identity with values, norms, and symbols that may span many organizations within or across multiple fields. This type of socialization facilitates acquisition of the skills, knowledge, and attitudes necessary to fulfill the duties of this role" (pp. 615–616).

As Chong, Ling, and Chuan (2011) state, a professional identity is developed over time and is formed through insights gained from learning about and applying the values, skills, and knowledge required and practiced as a member of the profession. International service learning allows pre-service teachers to construct and develop their identities as future teachers, especially working with diverse student populations. ISL helps them reflect that they are not only teachers but learners as well—learners of language, culture, people, and community.

This study is significant in that it addresses a dearth in the ISL and TESOL literature. In our survey of the literature, we did not come across an implementation of such an ISL program for pre- and in-service teachers. This study also evidences the effectiveness of ISL and its impact on professional teacher identities and intercultural competence.

## THE STUDY

This case study explores three pre-service teachers who fit within the dominant demographic aforementioned and how the ISL experience helped form their teacher professional identity and shape the dispositional characteristics that facilitate meaningful engagement with their future culturally and linguistically diverse students. Making this mostly implicit and hidden process explicit is crucial. As Kayi-Aydar (2015) suggests, "While it is important for teacher educators to understand what identities novice teachers construct, it is also crucial for them to understand why and how those identities are constructed" (p. 101)

This study mainly focuses on *how* these identities and knowledge are constructed in an international service-learning context. The central research question for this study was, How does an international service-learning experience help in forming the professional identity of mainstream pre-service teachers?

### Site Selection as the Context for International Service Learning

The location of the ISL experience was Naples, Italy. Naples was selected as the site because the lead author had a contact named Kelly (pseudonyms for real names are used throughout), an American who had been living in Naples for nine years at the time of the study. She knew the local community quite well and was considered an *insider*, liked and respected by the locals. Her being invested in the community provided access to everything *local*. This was very important as the goal for participating pre- and in-service teachers was to have an in-depth understanding and authentic experience of the local context.

An important point to note is that before setting up the service learning, the faculty traveled to Naples and conducted a needs assessment of the community, because when community needs are not taken into account, ISL programs can have negative effects on host communities. As Baker-Boosamra, Guevara, and Balfour (2006) have stated, "without community partners defining their own objectives for participation in service learning programs, the community becomes little more than a laboratory for the use of privileged students rather than being a true partner in learning" (p. 485).

Since the lead faculty of the program were bilingual/ESL education professors and the focus of the academic instruction was TESOL, the decision to teach EFL at a low-income public school was made (and a community in need was identified) after multiple meetings between the faculty and various schools, principals, and youth leaders appointed by the mayor of Naples. This was a unique opportunity for all participants because no U.S. university had gone to Naples and been involved with a local school teaching English before.

## Description of the Setting

The identified school was at the heart of the historic center in Naples, a neighborhood where 86% of the population did not attain higher than an elementary education and where youth potentially become gang recruits, according to a newspaper article (Falzon, 2006).

Most students in the neighborhood spoke Neapolitan as their first language rather than Italian. They spoke Neapolitan at home and learned Italian at school. According to Coluzzi (2008), Neapolitan is considered an "unsafe" (p. 220), close to an endangered dialect of Italian. He also discusses how in Neapolitan, "written materials exist, but they may only be useful for some members of the community; and for others, they may have a symbolic significance. Literacy education in the language is not a part of the school curriculum" (p. 221).

## Pre-Departure Preparation

Before leaving for Italy for summer 2015, throughout the 2014–2015 academic year, several informational meetings were provided about their involvement in Naples. EFL teaching methods and strategies, as well as lesson planning, were specifically taught through various workshops by the faculty who led the program because participating pre-service teachers did not have any teaching experience and the in-service teachers who were also part of the program did not have experience teaching EFL. In-service teachers had experience teaching English as a second language (ESL) instead.

## Setup of the International Service Learning

Before the faculty and students arrived, three local teachers at the participating school created a sign-up sheet for the "Summer Class in English." It was determined that the ISL project was going to be part of a summer school program at the local school as soon as the academic year ended. Close to 75 students (from grades 4, 5, and 6) signed up for the program voluntarily. This outcome resulted in six sections, with 10–12 students in each class.

The English classes ran from 9:00 a.m. until 12:00 p.m., Monday through Friday, for two weeks. Due to the pre-service teachers not having prior teaching experience, a co-teaching model, pairing a pre-service teacher with an in-service teacher who was a TESOL master's program student at the same university, was formed. Each day, each pair (co-teachers) created and taught a three-hour-long lesson based on the need and proficiency level of their students.

## Participants

A total of nine students participated in ISL. Five were undergraduate, and four were graduate students. Undergraduate students were studying in an early childhood through grade 6 (EC-6) program. While in Naples, they were enrolled in a junior level "Second Language Acquisition" course. Graduate students were studying TESOL. They were enrolled in a "Second Language Teaching" course. Three undergraduate students representing the predominant future teacher demographics in the United States (White, female, monolingual, and middle class) were selected for this study.

Tiffany was 20, Kate 20, and Lindsay 23 years old. Tiffany had not left the United States or her home state until this experience. Kate had traveled outside of the United States yet only with her parents, and Lindsay had traveled abroad but only on cruise ships.

## Data Collection and Analysis

This study consisted of a single-case design with multiple participants, since our participants shared many common characteristics and conditions (Merriam, 2009). There were two data sources: (1) reflection journals pre-during-post ISL and (2) semi-structured interviews after returning to the United States. The interviews allowed for detailed and deeper responses. All participant interviews were audio-recorded and transcribed. The data were coded and repeatedly reviewed until themes and patterns that answered our research question emerged (Boyatzis, 1998).

## FINDINGS

The designed experience included an overseas (the international component) setting in which pre-service teachers worked in a low-income public school with an opportunity to engage in meaningful community service (the service-learning component) and reflection. Similar to a practicum, the impact of well-structured experiences such as this one becomes evident when the pre-service teachers reflected on their participation and what it meant for their growing professional identity development.

The perceived impact can be evidenced by the following themes: gains in personal confidence and intercultural competence, professional teacher identity as a result of co-teaching, and participation within a community of practice. Each aspect will be discussed in detail below.

### New Gains in Personal Confidence and Intercultural Competence

Confidence, or self-esteem, is defined in this paper as a set of internalized feelings or an overall attitude about the self and one's perception of his or her value in society. While it is beyond the scope of this chapter to address self-esteem development in teacher training programs, it is clear that internalized value is an important variable for those in the role of a teacher.

For example, Lindsay was initially apprehensive about the experience, but her growing confidence seemed to arise from accomplishing her professional duties within the context of the experience. She even made a distinction between personal and professional confidence in saying, "I did not think it [ISL and teaching experience] would impact me like that. . . . I felt like so accomplished . . . confidence for me and as a teacher." During the interview, Kate noted jokingly how she had matured "because I didn't have my parents there to hold my hand all the time, I mean I had you all [faculty] but it wasn't just my parents, and so I was more independent." Since Tiffany has never been out of the United States before, she said,

> Before the experience, I was really intimidated and nervous but I was excited, and I didn't know what to expect. . . . Just the fact that I've never traveled by myself without any of my family members . . . definitely gained that experience and now . . . now that I want to go and travel by myself I know I can do it, I am more capable.

In all cases, pre-service teachers' personal confidence came as a result of performing the work—in essence, the *doing* of it. This suggests that confidence can be acquired through the engagement of the act.

Regarding gains in intercultural competence, Kate spoke of the traditional benefits of ISL experiences when she said, "The fact that we got to see a totally different culture was something that we gained because it is important to see other cultures to make yourself a more well-rounded person."

For Tiffany, she discussed the concept of intercultural competence as she made parallel connections between Italian and American schools and students. She said, "I think there is a really great need everywhere for teachers to pursue those kids who aren't just gonna sit in class . . . that same need is here, every school that we have here, I bet there are neighborhoods like that one (in Italy) in Houston, and being able to see that there, kind of put it in front of me that there is that here, too."

For Lindsay, connections to intercultural competence were evidenced when she said, "seeing that struggles like this do happen outside of the United States. If you just stayed here, I think people are in a bubble."

In a globalizing society, to have globally aware teachers, pre-service teachers need to have global experiences. ISL is one way to achieve this by connecting the local to the global.

## Teacher Professional Identity from Co-Teaching

The complex processes of identity formation are not only a critical part of human development but impact other areas of our lives, such as our careers and the professional identities we maintain within them. Professional identity is defined "as a description, or representation, of the self within specific professional practices" (Hicks, 2014, p. 252).

While many of our identifications in groups are somewhat decided for us at an early age, such as gender, racial/ethnic, or cultural identity, our professional identities begin to develop as we start to participate in a professional, career-oriented environment. They are shaped and reshaped by new experiences and understandings that must mingle with what is already known and influence currently held values, beliefs, and skills. This process of (re)construction continues until we retire or leave the profession.

Professional identity has been considered as an important aspect of teacher education since the early 2000s (Lamote & Engels, 2010), and for very good reason. The characteristics one has as part of their professional identity are likely to "determine the way teachers teach" (Lamote & Engels, 2010, p. 3). As Watson (2006) noted, "the links between identity, knowledge and practice is found more specifically in the assumption that *who we think we are* influences *what we do*" (Watson, 2006, p. 510).

The ISL experience provided the opportunity for the pre-service teachers to see themselves as international teachers, integrating their professional identity with a culturally competent element and global extension. All of the pre-service teachers' growth as professionals in the classroom came as a result of their lived experience engaging in the professional duties of a teacher. As Kate said,

> My co-teacher was amazing which made the experience even better. I have learned so much from this experience. Not only did I learn a little about the classroom management side of teaching, I also learned a lot about the planning side. Having Holly as a co-teacher who is a Special Ed teacher was a great thing. I learned so much about what she does in her classroom, and she gave me tips about what I can do in my future classroom.

Having never taught before, Lindsay initially expressed apprehension and potential embarrassment about "failing" and not being perceived by the students as a teacher. She said, "On Monday I was like, ohh my Lord, I am gonna fail. . . . I was like, they are gonna come in here and say, 'You are, no, you are not a teacher.' This is embarrassing, Lindsay, you can't." However, through the experience, her apprehension turned to confidence as she explained,

> This experience has already changed me so much as a future teacher. Before the class, I felt terrified and afraid of messing up in front of the students and Ana [her co-teacher]. As the class began and started, I loosened up and realized there was absolutely nothing to be afraid about! I feel so much more confident in my abilities and am so excited to start this new week with activities and lessons that Ana and I have started to come up with!

Tiffany's engagement in teaching merged with her sense of personal confidence and professional identity when she stated she was "a bit intimidated, thinking that I do not look much older than some of them. By the time the students came in and sat down, however, I was fine. It was a normal classroom of kids who want to learn." Later, she said, "After the class, I was very encouraged because I felt I could identify the problems that we had during the day and correct them the next lesson. I immensely enjoyed teaching these children," and "when the students were having fun and following instructions, I felt successful." The reflections by the pre-service teachers demonstrate how their professional identities grew by being engaged in the act of *doing*.

## Participation within a Community of Practice

Teaching EFL in a low-income school in a rough neighborhood introduced the pre-service teachers to an unfamiliar world and helped them make connections to their future teaching and potential culturally and linguistically diverse students they may have in their U.S. classroom. The unfamiliarity can spark an emotional response that (hopefully) facilitates a growth in empathy.

The discomfort felt at the end of one's comfort zone, as Adams, Bell, and Griffin (2007) argue, puts the student in the best place from which he or she can expand understanding, consider different perspectives and views, and broaden his or her awareness. Tiffany's experience being a language learner in a country where she did not speak the language of the majority arose when she recalled, "It was really frustrating with the kids, trying to communicate with the kids sometimes because *they* were really trying hard to communicate back with us."

Kate was also able to make comparisons between communicating with students from another language background who did not have special needs and her future special education students who may come to her with different needs and abilities. Communication was a focal point for her as she said, "Children that have special needs can't always communicate in the same way that children that don't have special needs can, and so I think the fact that I was put in a classroom where I had to communicate in so many different ways is going to help me with special education because the kids are not always going to get it the first time." This striking parallel between her ISL class and her future special education classroom is indicative of a meaningful, transformative learning experience (Taylor, 2008).

Throughout this study, pre-service teachers also brought up the idea of co-teaching within the community of practice, reporting multiple benefits for themselves and their future students. Additionally, the transferability to their own classroom was a powerful indicator of growing cultural competence in learning to work with their future diverse students and other benefits related to professional knowledge and skill. As a result of their participation within a community of practice, the co-teaching experience was deemed helpful by the pre-service teachers regarding gaining teacher competence. Kate, referring to her co-teacher, said,

> She [Holly] knew what she was doing so she kinda would implement that and then she would slowly let us kinda take over as the week went on so I really liked having her cuz she was like someone to look up to for sure, and I learned a lot from her, and she would always tell us after that like "you can do this, but like this was really good," so that was really nice.

In this mentor-mentee relationship, Kate regarded Holly as a role model. Tiffany said about her co-teaching experience, "After the class, I was very encouraged because I felt I could identify the problems that we had during the day and correct them the next lesson. I immensely enjoyed teaching these children." Lindsay understood that learning to teach is a progression. "I am patient with the kids and really eager to listen and understand them but need to work on things such as organization and classroom management. I know these things will take time to learn and perfect, but that is what teaching is all about!" The co-teaching model employed impacted the pre-service teachers' growing professional knowledge and skill within a community of practice.

## DISCUSSION AND IMPLICATIONS OF THE STUDY

The overall goal of the ISL program was to support and develop pre- and in-service teachers' understanding of diversity, social justice, and as a result hope that it leads to advocacy. The goal of this particular study was to examine how the ISL experience would help pre-service teachers in forming their professional teacher identities as well as their understanding of intercultural competence. The authors' belief is that experiences in an ISL setting became a catalyst in helping pre-service teachers shape or reshape their personal as well as professional identity.

The lead faculty of the program specifically wanted to provide the service learning at a low-income public school. Petrón and Ates (2015) in their study took a group of pre- and in-service teachers to study abroad in Costa Rica and noted, "We believed that opportunities to engage fully with issues of social justice were more likely to occur in a public school setting" (p. 77). Therefore, they chose schools that served significant numbers of children of Nicaraguan immigrants. Just like the Nicaraguan immigrant children in Costa Rica, the Neapolitan-speaking children in this particular neighborhood were marginalized in various ways due to their language and socioeconomic status.

All three pre-service teachers reflected on the challenges and celebrations of developing and teaching effective EFL lessons, communication strategies, and stages of second language acquisition. From their reflections, it was also apparent that experiential learning opportunities had a great impact on their overall experiences related to teaching. As Lindsay noted,

> I've never been on the other side of teaching before, I mean I observed and stuff, but you don't really do anything when you observe, so to be like, me, they are asking me the questions, and I had to come up with answers.

While observing and observation experiences are designed to elicit learning and can be valuable on their own, Lindsay's quote exemplifies the power of experiential learning. Cushner (2007) also supports the significant role experience plays:

> Schooling in general, and teacher education in particular, continues to address culture learning primarily from a cognitive orientation. That is, students read, watch films, listen to speakers, observe in classrooms and hold discussions around issues of cultural difference. This continues in spite of the growing body of research that demonstrates the critical role that experience plays in enhancing intercultural development. (p. 27)

ISL appeared to promote a sense of intercultural competence within the teacher candidates. The idea that we are more than members of our local communities, reaching beyond the borders of our state and/or country, has shown up in research on the importance of intercultural communication (Deardorff, 2006), the internationalizing of curriculum (Leask, 2013), and scholarship on study abroad experiences (Tarrant, Rubin, & Stoner, 2014). For programs and universities interested in incorporating an international outlook, ISL promotes a way to achieve this initiative.

Through this international practicum experience, co-teaching became a vehicle for pre-service teachers to actively participate in the tasks of teaching. It is through the doing of—the participating in and contributing to the community—that one gains the skills and competence to teach. It was evidenced through co-teaching that the pre-service teachers' sense of their identities as future professionals grew. Admittedly, the biggest challenge facing educators is getting students to apply what they are learning to life outside the classroom, toward meaningful and lasting outcomes. The authors of this study believe that ISL is a means for creating the lifelong learner.

## CONCLUSION

One may question why Naples and not an ISL program in a developing country? The answer is, "Why not?" As long as there is a neighborhood or school in need and a passionate local contact, Naples could be replaced with any place. It would not be fair to create a dichotomy between developed (developed countries have underresourced communities as well) and developing countries and discuss how participating individuals (both U.S. students and local community) could benefit from a similar experience more than the other. However, it is also extremely important for the faculty to affirm that wherever American students go they do not view themselves as *saviors*, the privileged Americans saving the underprivileged students around the world.

Unfortunately, due to financial constraints, not all pre-service teachers can go abroad. Therefore, TESOL faculty could create local service-learning opportunities in schools or communities where there are a high number of ESL students. However, if pre-service teachers could afford ISL programs, it is a rare experience that could help them grow and transform personally and professionally.

In conclusion, it is our belief that through ISL pre-service teachers learned more than any textbook could offer. ISL experiences expand the borders of students whose skills working with diverse populations will only become more necessary. We believe this is a model that can be replicated not only among teacher education programs but across disciplines in the United States and worldwide.

# REFERENCES

Adams, M., Bell, L. A., & Griffin, P. (2007). *Teaching for diversity and social justice.* New York: Routledge.

Baker-Boosamra, M., Guevara, J. A., & Balfour, D. L. (2006). From service to solidarity: Evaluation and recommendations for international service learning. *Journal of Public Affairs Education, 12*(4), 479–500.

Bamber, P. (2015). Becoming other-wise: Transforming international service-learning through nurturing cosmopolitanism. *Journal of Transformative Education, 13*(1), 26–45.

Bamber, P. M. (2016). *Transformative education through international service-learning: Realising an ethical ecology of learning.* New York: Routledge.

Boyatzis, R. E. (1998). *Transforming qualitative information: Thematic analysis and code development.* Thousand Oaks, CA: Sage.

Bringle, R. G., & Hatcher, J. A. (2011). International service learning. In R. G. Bringle, J. A. Hatcher, & S. G. Jones (Eds.), *International service learning: Conceptual frameworks and research* (pp. 3–28); IUPUI Series on Service Learning Research. Sterling, VA: Stylus.

Brody, J., Vissa, J., & Weathers, J. (2010). School leader professional socialization: The contribution of focused observations. *Journal of Research on Leadership Education, 5*(14), 611–651.

Buysse, V., Sparkman, K., & Wesley, P. (2013). Communities of practice: Connecting what we know with what we do. *Exceptional Children, 69*(3), 263–277.

Chong, S., Ling, L. W., & Chuan, G. K. (2011). Developing student teachers' professional identities—an exploratory study. *International Education Studies, 4*(1), 30–38.

Coluzzi, P. (2008). Language planning for Italian regional languages ("dialects"). *Language Problems & Language Planning, 32*(3), 215–236.

Crabtree, R. D. (2008). Theoretical foundations for international service learning. *Michigan Journal of Community Service Learning, 15*(1), 18–36.

Craigen, L. M., & Sparkman, N. M. (2014). The value and importance of international service learning programs: A model for human service education. *Journal of Human Services, 34*(1), 126–130.

Cushner, K. (2007). The role of experience in the making of internationally-minded teachers. *Teacher Education Quarterly, 34,* 27–39.

Danielson, C. (2016). Creating communities of practice. *Educational Leadership, 73*(8), 18–23.

Deardorff, D. (2006). Identification and assessment of intercultural competence as student outcome of internationalization. *Journal of Studies in International Education, 10*(3), 241–266.

Falzon, P. (2006, April 6). In Naples, the Camorra still prospers on poverty. *l'Humanité.* Retrieved from http://www.humaniteinenglish.com/article191.html.

Fitts, S., & Gross, L. A. (2012). Teacher candidates learning about and learning from English learners: Constructing concepts of language and culture in the Tuesdays' tutors afterschool program. *Teacher Education Quarterly, 39*(4), 75–95.

Frey, W. (2015). *Diversity explosion: How new racial demographics are remaking America.* Washington, DC: Brookings Institution Press.

Green, W., Hibbins, R., Houghton, L., & Ruutz, A. (2013). Reviving praxis: Stories of continual professional learning and practice architectures in a faculty-based teaching community of practice. *Oxford Review of Education, 39*(2), 247–266.

Haddix, M. (2015). Preparing community-engaged teachers. *Theory into Practice, 54*(1), 63–70.

Hicks, D. (2014). The construction of librarians' professional identities: A discourse analysis. *Canadian Journal of Information and Library Science, 38*(4), 251–270.

Kayi-Aydar, H. (2015). Teacher agency, positioning, and English language learners: Voices of pre-service classroom teachers. *Teaching and Teacher Education, 45,* 94–103.

Lamote, C., & Engels, N. (2010). The development of student teachers' professional identity. *European Journal of Teacher Education, 33*(1), 3–18.

Larsen, M. (2014). Critical global citizenship and international service learning: A case study of the intensification effect. *Journal of Global Citizenship and Equity Education, 4*(1), 1–41.

Lave, J., & Wenger, E. (1991). *Situated learning: Legitimate peripheral participation.* Cambridge: Cambridge University Press.

Leask, B. (2013). Internationalizing the curriculum in the disciplines—Imagining new possibilities. *Journal of Studies in International Education, 17*(2), 103–118.

Li, L., Grimshaw, J. M., Nielsen, C., Judd, M., Coyte, P. C., & Graham, I. D. (2009). Evolution of Wenger's concept of community of practice. *Implementation Science, 4*(11).

Merriam, S. B. (2009). *Qualitative research: A guide to design and implementation.* San Francisco, CA: Jossey-Bass.

Miller, K. K., & Gonzalez, A. M. (2010). Domestic and international service learning experiences: A comparative study of preservice teacher outcomes. *Issues in Educational Research, 20*(1), 29–38.

National Forum on Education Statistics. (2016). *Forum guide to collecting and using disaggregated data on racial/ethnic subgroups.* (NFES 2017-017). U.S. Department of Education. Washington, DC: National Center for Education Statistics.

Neal, L. V. I, Sleeter, C. E., & Kumashiro, K. K. (2015). Introduction: Why a diverse teaching force must thrive. In C. Sleeter, L. V. I., Neal, & K. K. Kumashiro (Eds.), *Diversifying the teacher workforce: Preparing and retaining highly effective teachers* (pp. 1–16). New York: Routledge.

Nistor, N., Daxecker, I., Stanciu, D., & Diekamp, O. (2015). Sense of community in academic communities of practice: Predictors and effects. *Higher Education, 69,* 257–273.

Petrón, M., & Ates, B. (2015). Culture and class: Latina preservice teachers in Costa Rica. In D. Schwarzer & B. L. Bridglall (Eds.), *Promoting global competence and social justice in teacher education* (pp. 71–90). Lanham, MD: Lexington Books.

Pettit, S. (2011). Teachers' beliefs of English language learners in the mainstream classroom: A review of literature. *International Multicultural Research Journal, 5*(2), 123–147.

Rodríguez, E. (2011). What preservice teachers bring home when they travel abroad: Rethinking teaching through a short international immersion experience. *Scholar-Practitioner Quarterly, 5*(3), 289–305.

Schmitz, S. A., Nourse, S. W., & Ross, M. E. (2013). Increasing teacher diversity: Growing your own through partnerships. *Education Digest, 78*(5), 59–63.

Sharma, S., Rahatzad, J., & Phillion, J. (2013). How preservice teachers engage in the process of (de)colonization: Findings from an international field experience in Honduras. *Interchange, 43,* 363–377.

Tarrant, M., Rubin, D. L., Stoner, L. (2014). The added value of study abroad: Fostering a global citizenry. *Journal of Studies in International Education, 18*(2), 141–161.

Taylor, E. W. (2008). Transformative learning theory. In S. B. Merriam (Ed.), *Third update on adult learning theory* (pp. 5–15). New directions of adult and continuing education, no. 119. San Francisco, CA: Jossey-Bass.

Vatalaro, A., Szente, J., & Levin, J. (2015). Transformative learning of pre-service teachers during study abroad in Reggio Emilia, Italy: A case study. *Journal of the Scholarship of Teaching and Learning, 15*(2), 42–55.

Watson, C. (2006). Narratives of practice and the construction of identity in teaching. *Teachers and Teaching, 12*(5), 509–526.

*Chapter Eight*

# Online Service Learning

*Learning Beyond the Classroom*

## Jin Young Choi

Over the past decade, higher education has experienced notable changes. With the increasing importance of a post-secondary degree in the labor market, higher numbers of non-traditional and part-time students and those who seek professional development and credentials came back to school. According to the 2015 National Center for Education Statistics (NCES) report (Radford, Cominole, & Skomsvold, 2015), about 74% of undergraduate students of the 2011–2012 academic year were non-traditional students, who were often characterized as independent for financial aid purposes, having one or more dependents, being a single caregiver, not having a traditional high school diploma, having delayed post-secondary enrollment, having attended school part-time, and being employed full-time (Brock, 2010; Choy, 2002).

The post-secondary education costs for all institutions, including public and private institutions, have increased more than 28% after adjusting for inflation between the 2003–2004 and 2013–2014 academic years (Snyder, de Brey, & Dillow, 2016). Fast-rising educational expenses pressured higher education institutions to reduce costs (Bartley & Golek, 2004). At the same time, higher education institutions increasingly endorsed the value of educating students about the importance of responsible citizenship and have facilitated their civic engagement in social change.

With these heightened needs related to the changes in the academic environment, higher education institutions have recognized the importance of online instruction and service learning that integrates academic instruction with community engagement. They have increasingly provided online education as a learning option for students and an essential part of academic instruction (Bartley & Golek, 2004; De la Varre, Keane, & Irvin, 2011; Gratton-Lavoie & Stanley, 2009).

According to the 2010 Sloan Survey of Online Learning based on more than 2,500 colleges and universities in the United States (Allen & Seaman, 2010), 63% of schools reported that online education is a critical part of their future class offerings, and almost 30% of all student enrollments are currently in online courses. Service learning is considered as a useful pedagogical tool, which enriches students' academic learning experience and develops their social responsibilities and leadership through civic engagement. It also strengthens communities and fulfills the mission of the institution by greater collaboration between the university and the surrounding communities (McGorry, 2012).

As more students seek online education as an alternative to classroom learning and higher education institutions realize the benefits of service learning in academic instruction, interest in integrating service learning and online instruction will continue to increase (Allen & Seaman, 2011). However, there are limited studies on implementation and learning outcomes of online service learning in sociology (Eudey, 2012).

This chapter illustrates an example of online service learning in a four-year college in the southern region of the United States and examines the effects of online service learning on the students' learning outcomes, particularly in the discipline of sociology. It also identifies challenges that students have faced in an integral course of online service learning. The remainder of this chapter discusses the methods, course description, results, and implications of online service learning after reviewing the literature on online education and service learning.

## Online Education

Online education has gained an increasing presence because of its reported benefits, including flexibility and cost effectiveness. Online education addresses the needs of students who do not have access to traditional on-campus programs or a classroom setting. Many of these students are non-traditional students who are constrained by distance, time, and family and/or work responsibilities (Li & Irby, 2008). Online education provides these students with opportunities to reach the tools to empower themselves through its geographical and temporal flexibility (Cornford & Pollock, 2003). For example, the removal of travel time and costs associated with learning in the traditional classroom setting significantly reduces expenses driven by time lost and excused responsibilities at home and work. Online education also provides a *learner-centered environment*, allowing students more control with pacing and sequencing in a course and the ability to adapt their learning styles using many available online tools (Bartley & Golek, 2004; Clarke & Hermens, 2001).

Furthermore, online education is considered as an effective way to resist the increasing cost of higher education. There is a fringe cost for a student to take online courses. However, the overall expense of education can be reduced by spreading the cost of a class over a larger number of students compared to the traditional classroom setting, which has more constraints such as the size and availability of physical classroom space (Bartley & Golek, 2004; Bowen, 2013; Jung & Rha, 2000).

With the significant growth and importance of online education, a debate around its effectiveness as a learning tool has emerged. Ensuring quality and efficacy of online education has become increasingly important (Driscoll et al., 2012). However, limited rigorous research efforts have been made to provide empirical evidence concerning online education (Lack, 2013), and studies present inconsistent findings.

Nguyen (2015) concluded in the review of previous studies that online education has robust effectiveness at least equal to a traditional classroom format in terms of three aspects: its effectiveness, the heterogeneous outcomes of student learning, and endogenous issues pertaining to learning environment choice (online vs. traditional classroom setting). In the study of Hannay and Newvine (2006) on students' perceptions of online education, students perceived that they achieved higher-quality learning outcomes in the online setting than in a traditional format. More than half of students (57%) reported that they learned more in the online setting. In contrast, Lack's meta-analysis (2013) showed little evidence that online instruction was significantly more effective or less effective than traditional classroom instruction.

## Service Learning

Putnam (2000) emphasized the role of higher education in civic engagement in response to a perceived civic decline. Higher education institutions have recognized the importance of service learning that integrates academic instruction with community engagement (Howard, 1998; Center for Community Engagement, 2017). Substantial research efforts have been made to examine service learning as a pedagogical innovation to enrich student learning (Kiely, 2005).

The positive rhetoric on the efficacy of service learning for students has been supported by empirical evidence. For example, in the study of more than 600 students taking service-learning courses in 30 different disciplines, Levesque-Bristol and colleagues (2010) found that community engagement had a significant positive effect on the learning climate, motivation, civic skills, problem solving, communication, critical analysis skills, and appreciation of diversity. Service learning also helps students elevate morale and awareness of social issues, heighten values regarding service and commitment to help others, and develop a variety of personal skills. Moreover, students can develop an enhanced sense of community and social responsibility through community engagement (Astin & Sax, 1998; Calleson, Jordan, & Seifer, 2005; Densmore, 2000).

Service learning is particularly relevant to the discipline of sociology. Mills argued that the "sociological imagination has its chance to make a difference in the quality of human life" (Mills, 1959/2000, p. 226). Students in sociology are expected to exercise their "sociological imagination" beyond the classroom to see the world through a more critical perspective and view themselves as agents for social change, who are embedded in social, structural, and historical contexts (Mills, 1959/2000). Mobley (2007) argued that service learning facilitates students' understanding of the sociological imagination and the effects of structural forces on individuals. Petray and Halbert (2013) indicated "engagement and social justice as key outcomes of a sociology degree within the broader context of the changing higher education sector" (p. 441) and stated that "encouraging active engagement through classroom practice is a successful means of fostering students' capacity to think sociologically" (p. 446).

Despite its potential benefits, service-learning pedagogy is *counter-normative* (Clayton & Ash, 2004; Howard, 1998) and requires significant shifts in content, activities, format, delivery methods, roles of faculty (e.g., as a resource and facilitator who supports students' experiential learning) and students, their relationship with community stakeholders, criteria for evaluation, and the learning process. Such shifts can lead faculty, students, administrators, and community organizations to be confused on both personal and professional levels (Clayton & Ash, 2004). Thus, it is vital for successful service learning to incorporate careful planning before its implementation (e.g., different components of the service learning project, building relationships and interacting with the community partners), as well as to help students obtain a better understanding of course content and learning goals (Berman, 2006).

The effectiveness of service learning can vary by previous service-learning experience, implementation method, type of involvement, level of motivation, and connectedness to organization and projects (Brandes & Randall, 2011; Levesque-Bristol et al., 2010; Parker-Gwin & Mabry, 1998).

On the other hand, Butin (2010) argued that service learning is "an embodied experiential activity" (p. 46), and it cannot be a neat learning experience that leaves some people behind after every service-learning experience. Students' time constraints, anxiety related to community experiences, and the limitations of participating organizations hinder instructors from accomplishing what they intended, and this results in inherent slippages (Butin, 2010;

Rose, 1989). Thus, it is important to understand that learning outcomes are not immaculate and there is a wide range of possible responses to service learning (Petray & Halbert, 2013).

An integral format of online service learning could provide students unique opportunities for a learning experience focused on real-world problems (Guthrie & McCracken, 2010). Waldner and colleagues (2012) argued that an online format of service learning is "a key to the future of service-learning" (p. 123) because of its potential to provide great flexibility from place-based access or geographical constraints. Several studies have documented many successful cases of integrating service learning and online instruction across the disciplines (Blackwell, 2008; Guthrie & McCracken, 2010; Ralph & McNeal, 2012; Waldner, McGorry, & Widener, 2012). For example, McNeal (2012) found that an online format was at least as effective as the traditional classroom format in service learning. In terms of students' perceived service-learning benefits, there was no significant difference between a traditional classroom format and an online format (McGorry, 2012). However, there are limited studies on implementation and learning outcomes of online service learning in sociology (Eudey, 2012).

## METHODS

### Research Design

The study discussed in this chapter employs a case study approach to understand service learning delivered in an online format and to explore the effects of an integral course of service learning and online instruction on student learning and their perceived challenges. A case study is a research design often employed to explore new trials with limited information, to concentrate on experiential knowledge and contextual influences, and to allow the use of a variety of informational sources (e.g., documents, interviews, observations) (Yin, 2013).

According to Stake (2005), a case study approach is appropriate when the goal is to understand a particular case in a specific context and to provide insights about a broad issue. Given the purpose of this study and its setting that is limited to one course, a case study approach is an appropriate research method for this study. In order to understand practical strategies of implementation and contextual influences in a case study, it is important to describe and explore a service-learning course delivered in an online format (Guthrie & McCracken, 2010). Multiple sources, including the course syllabus, student reflection essays, journals, discussions, and the final project, were used to describe the course and assess the student learning outcomes and the challenges that students faced.

## Students in the Course

There were 12 students enrolled in the course at the time of the study, 17% of whom had previously taken at least one service-learning course at the institution. The student characteristics of the class were 92% female, 50% non-White, 67% sociology major or minors, 92% juniors or seniors, and 75% non-traditional students. Three-quarters of students were working at least 20 hours per week. During the school year all of them lived off campus, with 71.4% residing outside of the county in which the school is located. This residence pattern is a good reflection of the characteristics of online students who seek flexibility from geographical constraints associated with traditional courses taught in the classroom.

## Course Description

An elective undergraduate sociology course at a four-year university in the southern region of the United States was used as a case to study. At the time of the study, it was offered as an integral course of service learning and online instruction. Thus, an online platform was utilized to provide the course instruction and most course communication, which included e-mail communication with students and the instructor, discussion boards, and notification of upcoming deadlines. For online students, the university provides an orientation on how to operate and interact in the online platform environment and how to access course materials, communicate with classmates and the professor, submit assignments, take tests, and check grades.

The course was a medical sociology course, which was designed to introduce to students the social aspects of health, illness, and the health-care system, with a focus on social inequalities, social determinants, and social construction of health and illness. Community engagement was required to help students extend their learning beyond the classroom, encouraging them to consider themselves as a positive force in the world and gain a deeper understanding of their role as a citizen.

The service-learning component of the course is called the ECHO (Engagement of Community Health Organizations) project. Students' voluntary engagement in community organizations (ECHO) formed the basis for observations of health and health-care issues among different segments of the population (e.g., gender, age, racial/ethnic, cultural, social class groups) in society. In addition, various course activities related to community engagement (e.g., pre- and post-reflections; two journals during community engagement; various discussions about perceptions of service learning, citizenship, social responsibility, social inequality in health and health care, and social forces determining health; and an ECHO portfolio) were utilized to help students better understand "the root causes of social problems" and inequalities that lead to injustice in the area of health and health care.

The ECHO project is composed of three major stages: (1) the project preparation stage, (2) the progress stage, and (3) the finale stage. Each stage consists of a series of several activities. Through an online instruction platform, the overall description of the ECHO project and its timelines were provided in the course syllabus, as well as a detailed set of instructions and a template for each activity based on the course schedule.

The preparation stage includes the following: (1) searching for and contacting non-profit health-related organizations/agencies in the students' neighborhoods or communities, (2) developing their own ECHO project plan and learning objectives, and (3) obtaining a service contract with the organization. In this preparation stage, the emphasis was placed on finding an eligible organization for the student and establishing a relationship between student and organization, as well as between the organization and the instructor.

Unlike a service-learning course in a traditional classroom setting, it was difficult to work with particular organizations in this online service-learning course because of the geographic dispersion of online students. Students were encouraged to find their community organizations by themselves in their local communities, even if some students worked with community organizations where the instructor has established a partnership through several years of teaching this service-learning course. Thus, it was important for students to have a clear understanding about the criteria for eligible community organizations: a non-profit organization that provides health and health-related services; has ongoing and/or incoming projects/events related to health, health care, and health services; and accepts volunteers. Through several monitoring procedures, students were ensured of their choice of an eligible community organization.

During the progress stage, students had to complete the required volunteer hours (15 hours) and submit their time sheets and logs. In addition, reflections, journals, and threaded discussions were utilized during the preparation and progress stages to promote critical thinking, reflection, and shared dialogue about the students' experiences and the learning process involved in community engagement.

Along with Devers's study (2011) about the effectiveness of the use of discussions in an online service-learning course, a discussion board was frequently used in this course. In an initial discussion, students were asked to share their background, which could help better understand students' values, perceptions, and experiences related to civic engagement, as well as the community and social issues, in line with Ashworth and Bourelle's (2014) suggestion. During the semester, students were prompted to actively participate in discussions to cultivate their deeper understanding of critical issues.

Eyler (2001) suggested reflection-based activities before, during, and after students' community engagement as a useful strategy. Students in the course were required to write reflections and journals to assess their experience, lessons they had learned, changes in their perspectives and the broader implications that the service experience had on them, their learning, and their future plans, as well as the challenges that they faced. These additional ECHO-related activities were expected to inspire students' awareness about social problems and structural inequalities in health and health care and the importance of action for social change by providing opportunities to reconsider the value of service and the promotion of active learning (Ashworth & Bourelle, 2014).

In the final stage, students were asked to generate an ECHO portfolio, which includes a compilation of the following: the basic information and needs of the community that their organization serves; all the ECHO project activities; relevant academic works (theories and concepts) that they learned from the class; media coverage of the issues, services, and policies related to their engaged organization; and a plan for their action research or future projects. The ECHO portfolio represents a culmination of learning from the class materials and service experiences and provides sizable evidence of the students' development and achievement during the semester.

In particular, incorporation of academic content and media coverage of social issues related to their community engagement in the ECHO portfolio was designed to help students contextualize their classroom learning, challenge the status quo, and analyze social inequalities driven by power structures in their own contexts. Moreover, in order to assess each student's service and contributions to the organization and/or community, the organization supervisors were asked to evaluate each student's performance in their organization.

## RESULTS

### Initial Service-Learning Experience

In the reflections and class discussions that they submitted before they began their community service, most students reported that they valued volunteer service to the community and to society and that they enjoyed serving the community. They also believed that they had a responsibility to serve the community and that they could make a difference in their community through engagement. However, most students shared that they were not ready for community service even after they had almost one month of step-by-step class preparation for ECHO service. For example, a student stated in her first reflection essay, "Before starting this volunteering experience at the Boys and Girls Club, I was extremely nervous. I wasn't sure what I would be doing or who I would meet and what things could happen. I honestly was not ready."

## Experience of Service Learning

Students' learning outcomes from online service learning were presented in three main areas: academic learning of sociology, individual empowerment, and social responsibility.

### Academic Learning of Sociology

The process of obtaining new perspectives, connecting the sociology learned in the classroom to the real world, and the reinforcement and actualization of sociological insights were prominent outcomes from community engagement in the academic learning of sociology.

*Process of obtaining sociological perspectives.* It was common that students' stereotypes and prejudice toward unprivileged populations were challenged and changed during their service experience. One student expressed, "This was a good challenge of my assumptions and stereotypes." Another student stated, "I've briefly described my past prejudices, thanks to this organization those conceptions have been cleared away. . . . I'm happy to say that now I've dropped the predisposition and consider myself educated about the clientele." One other student shared the following:

> Through this experience I have learned one very valuable lesson: There is a world filled with homeless and low income families around me that is much larger and goes much deeper than I ever thought possible. Never again will I look at the homeless man selling papers or holding a sign at a stoplight in the same way.

Students also gained sociological perspectives through their community service experiences. For instance, one student noted, "The ECHO Project experience was an incredibly positive experience that allowed me a number of insights that I would have been difficult to acquire without this specific opportunity." More specifically, students reported that they became aware of existing inequalities in health and health care across different social groups and perceived the inequalities as institutionalized structures. One student shared, "Visit a homeless shelter, a free clinic, or even a publically funded health fair. The gap between the quality of service the people at those places are getting compared to commercial or private insurance patients is astonishing." Another student said, "My experience brought many questions that I never considered. Many people that are infected with HIV/AIDS are disproportionately African Americans and they have no voice and no advocate. . . .

This to me means that dying from HIV is a community issue not a personal one."

*Connecting sociology to the real world.* Most students related theories and concepts that they learned from the class material to what they observed and experienced through service learning. Students reflected that their community engagement experiences helped them to connect theories with practice and to apply subject matter in a "real world" situation. One student wrote,

> In the context of this class, I was exposed to data and perceptions primarily concerning the social distribution of illness in the [name of the community] area, which closely mirrors the distribution of illness found across the county, as presented by Weitz (2013). The data for the [name of the community] area supports the fundamental-cause theory in that the health realities of those with restricted access to financial resources have decidedly lower health outcomes than those who have less restricted access to resources.

Another student shared this insight:

> As a volunteer for [name of organization], I have been exposed to some of the different sociological concepts and theories that make up this type of organization. My experience has allowed me to put forth the knowledge that I have learned through class material and I have been able to interpret not only why these things happen, but also who may be more prone to execute them.

*Reinforcement and actualization of learning.* Service-learning activities and projects extended students' learning beyond the classroom. Their understanding of the social aspects of health and the roles of social forces in health, as well as their awareness of existing inequalities in health and health care across different social groups were reinforced and actualized through their community engagement. One student stated, "I am a sociology student and have studied all the theories of exploitation and function, but this project has convinced me, more than any other previous experience, that change in our health care is needed." Another student reported, "My study within the sociology department leads me to challenge this 'common knowledge,' but this experience gave me personal experiences that validate the critical analysis of these kinds of stereotypes." One other student noted,

> With this experience I came to a better understanding of a class of citizens that I will most likely be focused on reaching. . . . By now understanding some of the trials they go through, and interacting with different people in time of crisis, I can safely say my understanding has been deepened. Also, I enjoy this sort of task. With a minor in sociology, any opportunity to step into the shoes of someone else is thoroughly exciting.

*Individual Empowerment*

Community engagement helps students to learn about themselves and to define their personal strengths and weaknesses. One student expressed, "Self-discovery wasn't a big event during this project." Another student said, "The service experience through volunteering has also built character in me rather than simply to perform specific tasks. It has not only strengthened my self-identity, but also has created a kind of identity that fits well with the demands and responsibilities of our society." Students also indicated that their self-confidence and maturity were elevated. One student revealed,

> My life has honestly been a roller coaster of ups and downs and I feel that my experience as a volunteer has brought me closer to my community, which in turn has brought me happiness. I feel as if I am now a more confident person and someone that can take on any challenge.

Another one said, "I feel like this experience has helped me grow as a person, seeing the need of others inspires me to go out and volunteer to help them out."

Students' practical skills and interpersonal skills were also improved through community engagement, and these prepared students better for the future. All of the students mentioned that community engagement helped enhance their leadership and critical thinking skills, as well as communication, organizational, and workplace skills. They believed that enhancement of these practical and interpersonal skills helped them to be employable and empowered them via elevated self-confidence and happiness.

Moreover, community engagement provides an opportunity for students to think about their future careers. One student revealed, "My experiences within the ECHO Project have created a level of interest that I am confident will manifest itself in the remainder of my education and my professional life as well." Another student shared how the service-learning experience shaped her specific career goal as well as her plans to achieve it. She said,

> I absolutely loved my experience and learned more about myself and what direction to take my career. They inspired me to want to choose a career that will help them [children]. I would really love to become a family advocate and pursue a master's degree and eventually become a counselor.

*Fostering Social Responsibility*

Students became more interested in and had better understanding about the needs and health issues of their community and the roles of social forces through community engagement. A student shared, "To understand our experiences in life, we must understand our historical period and the social forces that are sweeping the time in which we live, so by volunteering there, my viewpoint of [name of the community] was altered, and I was able to better understand my community."

At the same time, students realized the importance of practicing citizenship, and their social responsibility and belief in their ability to make a difference in their community were enhanced. One student said, "I also learned how it is important to give back to the community and help out the needy." Another student shared, "I have learned that by volunteering, you can make a difference for someone." Moreover, the service experience reified and exteriorized students' citizenship by facilitating their long-term commitment to their communities. A student said,

> Thank you for assigning this project because I have learned a lot about myself and my community. . . . I am happy to give back to my community and help my community the same way it helped me and my family when we needed help. I want to continue doing volunteer work for nonprofit organizations . . . so I can be able to explore more opportunities and encourage people to get more involved in giving back to the community.

## Challenges

Students experienced challenges in implementing logistics and achieving learning goals while taking the course. The challenges in logistics were directly related to the service-learning component: a time-consuming process and a sequential procedure. Service learning requires a substantial amount of time for initiating, processing, and completing community engagement. Students reported that it was a time-consuming process to find a relevant nonprofit organization, obtain the organization's permission and contract for volunteer work, and write journals and essays related to their ECHO activities. Due to the fact that online students are typically widely spread out in terms of their residence, only a few students were able to use the community partners that the instructor had established a relationship with. They had to search for an eligible organization, build relationships, and obtain permission by themselves, and this process was time consuming.

Service learning also involves a sequential process. Failing to complete one activity in time or falling behind made it difficult for students to keep up, particularly for those who had a full-time job or other commitments (e.g., taking multiple courses, family responsibilities). Despite the well-planned course schedule for service learning—early initiation of the process (within a week after the semester began), more than a month of step-by-step preparation (getting an agreement with an organization), and the instructor's flexibility for the completion period of service hours—several students who procrastinated with respect to the initiation and the preparation process had difficulty in catching up. Many students reported that they took this online class due to time flexibility, but the sequential and time-consuming nature of service learning limited the flexibility of online learning.

Organizational requirements and constraints were another challenge that students experienced in the logistics of community service. Some organizations required students to complete a background/criminal check before starting work due to the nature of the health-related work and vulnerability of the population they served (e.g., children, the elderly, low-income populations, the homeless). It increased processing time and generated emotional uneasiness for students (e.g., students who have a record of misdemeanors). Moreover, organizations often need students' service during the weekdays, while students wanted to and/or were able to work on the weekends. Students reported difficulty in scheduling their community service. This was particularly true for non-traditional students working part-time or full-time. Students also expressed anxiety related to difficulties in contacting their organization supervisors or the delayed response from their organizations due to organizational constraints (e.g., the lack of staff or staff changes in the organization, or an unorganized volunteer schedule).

In addition to the logistical challenges, students experienced difficulty in achieving their learning goals. Several students reported that they could not complete what the instructor had intended, and what they themselves had established, as learning goals set up through discussion with their organization supervisor at the preparation stage. This learning experience issue was closely related to the implementation challenge of the logistics.

Students expressed their difficulty in coordinating time to participate in the intended projects or activities in their organization because of other commitments such as long hours at work and family issues (e.g., child care). For example, one student, who was supposed to help at a health fair to learn about health disparities and the health-care needs of an underserved population, could not participate in the event due to an urgent family issue. Eventually, she just helped packing/labeling products because of the difficulty in coordinating her schedule with other organizational events and activities.

Students also indicated that their planned activities were compromised due to the organization's needs and the limited range of services that the organization actually offered the student to participate in. Many students often ended up doing clerical or sales work. For instance, one student reported that during her community service, she just sold clothes in a shop which was a part of the organization.

## SUMMARY AND CONCLUSIONS

This case study highlights the benefits and the challenges of service learning delivered in an online format for students' learning in the discipline of sociology. Students in the integral course of service learning and online instruction demonstrated positive learning outcomes, improved personal characteristics, and elevated citizenship. In terms of the students' learning, they experienced an increased awareness of social inequalities and social responsibility and changes in their perception and attitudes toward different social groups.

Students also gained sociological perspectives on community issues and social problems and demonstrated an improved ability to connect theories and concepts that they learned in the classroom to real-world situations. Their learning was reinforced and actualized as it extended beyond the classroom. Moreover, the service-learning opportunity empowered online students to discover more about themselves, ponder and prepare for their future careers, and improve various personal skills such as critical thinking, leadership, communication and interpersonal relationships, and other work-related skills. They gained deeper understandings of their roles as citizens and the importance of practicing citizenship. These findings are consistent with the findings of efficacy studies on service learning provided in a traditional classroom setting (Astin & Sax, 1998; Calleson et al., 2005) and in an online format (McGorry, 2012).

This case study particularly shows how an online service-learning pedagogical approach provides positive learning outcomes and critical perspectives in sociology. This sociology course was designed to introduce students to the social aspects of health, illness, and the health-care system, with an emphasis on social inequalities, social determinants, and social construction of health and illness. Through community engagement, students' stereotypes and preconceptions of unprivileged populations were challenged. They gained a sociological perspective about these groups and related social issues and realized the health inequalities embedded in social structure.

Despite its remarkable potential benefits, students experienced challenges inherent in the two core components of an online service-learning course—the nature of service learning (e.g., time-consuming process, sequential procedure) and the characteristics of online students (e.g., non-traditional students, students with more time and space constraints). Community engagement is time consuming particularly for online students. The community organizations that students are involved in are often located in their local communities. Online students searched for potential organizations in their local communities, built relationships with them, and got permission by themselves, instead of going to the community organizations that the instructor had built a partnership with. This process took time.

Considering that three-quarters of students were non-traditional students working at least 20 hours per week in addition to their school workload, securing time for preparation and actual engagement with organizations and coordinating schedules for community service activities are challenges for online students. Coupled with the characteristics of online students, they created anxiety and required additional efforts to reduce such logistical challenges for online students.

Moreover, the time constraints of these students, coupled with the limitations of the organizations themselves, often resulted in compromised service activities and the experience of "slippage" in service learning, as Butin (2010) has noted. Eventually, these factors become obstacles to achieving the learning goals that each student set up and that the instructor intended. This finding suggests that online education provides students flexibility from time and geographic constraints for taking classes, but not much flexibility when service learning is based on on-site participation.

There are a few limitations in this study. This case study examined only one type of delivery in service learning, and thus it is difficult to measure the efficacy of online delivery of service learning without comparing it to traditional classroom delivery. The investigation of the course occurred during the span of a single course and in one semester. Considering that it takes time for students to reflect perspectives forged in the course, it should be noted that the observed learning outcomes and challenges are limited to instant and short-term results.

In addition, this study focuses only on the benefits and challenges of online service learning experienced by students. This limitation stems from the scope of the chapter. Service learning involves several critical agents other than students. It is important to understand the potential benefits of service learning for these interest groups, including the community partner (useful outcomes), the instructor (service opportunities for tenure), and the university itself (positive community relations) (Waldner et al., 2012). However, this study limits its scope only to the students' learning outcomes. Thus, future studies should investigate the effects of service learning delivered in an online format on all parties involved.

Recently there has been a call for a more vigorous and critical approach to service learning. Mitchell (2008) argued that service learning should go beyond encouraging students to develop social responsibility, so-called *traditional service learning,* and focus on inequality and social justice—a *critical service learning* approach. Service learning should be reinvented as a more vigorous approach (e.g., organizational learning, community development, and research) beyond pedagogy because it could lead to more meaningful social change by promoting a democratizing and empowering approach to pedagogy (Swords & Kiely, 2010).

Several studies (e.g., Wang & Rodgers, 2006) have shown successful cases of critical service learning in the traditional classroom setting. As pedagogy is moved into an online format, it is important to address the online environment and provide ways to serve online students better, incorporating critical service learning. Further research is required to address these issues.

# REFERENCES

Allen, I. E., & Seaman, J. (2010, November). Class differences: Online education in the United States, 2010. Sloan Consortium (NJ1). Retrieved October 10, 2013, from http://sloanconsortium.org/publications/survey/class_differences.

Allen, I. E., & Seaman, J. (2011). Going the distance: Online education in the United States, 2011. Sloan Consortium. Retrieved October 10, 2013, from http://files.eric.ed.gov/fulltext/ED529948.pdf.

Ashworth, E., & Bourelle, T. (2014). Utilizing critical service-learning pedagogy in the online classroom: Promoting social justice and effecting change? *Currents in Teaching & Learning, 7,* 64–79.

Astin, A. W., & Sax, L. J. (1998). How undergraduates are affected by service participation. *Journal of College Student Development, 39,* 251–263.

Bartley, S. J., & Golek, J. H. (2004). Evaluating the cost effectiveness of online and face-to-face instruction. *Educational Technology & Society, 7*(4), 167–175.

Berman, S. (2006). *Service learning: A guide to planning, implementing, and assessing student projects.* Thousand Oaks, CA: Corwin Press.

Blackwell, C. W. (2008). Service-elearning: Meeting the objectives of community-based nursing education. In Amber Dailey-Hebert, Emily Donnelli Sallee, & Laurie N. Dipadova-Stocks (Eds.), *Service-elearning: Educating for citizenship* (pp. 87–94). Charlotte, NC: Information Age Publishing.

Bowen, W. G. (2013). *Higher education in the digital age.* Princeton, NJ: Princeton University Press.

Brandes, K., & Randall, K. (2011). Service learning and civic responsibility: Assessing aggregate and individual level change. *International Journal of Teaching and Learning in Higher Education, 23,* 20–29.

Brock, T. (2010). Young adults and higher education: Barriers and breakthroughs to success. *The Future of Children, 20,* 109–132.

Butin, D. (2010). *Service-learning in theory and practice: The future of community engagement in higher education.* Basingstoke: Palgrave Macmillan.

Calleson, D. C., Jordan, C., & Seifer, S. D. (2005). Community-engaged scholarship: Is faculty work in communities a true academic enterprise? *Academic Medicine, 80,* 317–321.

Center for Community Engagement, Sam Houston State University. (2017). *What is academic community engagement?* Retrieved from http://www.shsu.edu/academics/cce/ace/.

Choy, S. (2002). *Nontraditional undergraduates: Findings from the conditions of education 2002. NCES 2002–2012.* Washington, DC: U.S. Department of Education, National Center for Education Statistics. Retrieved October 15, 2016, from http://files.eric.ed.gov/fulltext/ED546117.pdf.

Clarke, T., & Hermens, A. (2001). Corporate developments and strategic alliances in e-learning. *Education + Training, 43,* 256–267.

Clayton, P. H., & Ash, S. L. (2004). Shifts in perspective: Capitalizing on the counter-normative nature of service-learning. *Michigan Journal of Community Service Learning, 11,* 59–70.

Cornford, J., & Pollock, N. (2003). *Putting the university online: Information, technology, and organizational change.* Buckingham, UK: Society for Research into Higher Education and Open University Press.

De la Varre, C., Keane, J., & Irvin, M. J. (2011). Enhancing online distance education in small rural US schools: A hybrid, learner-centred model. *Journal of Asynchronous Learning Networks, 15*(4), 35–46.

Densmore, K. (2000). Service learning and multicultural education: Suspect or transformative. In Carolyn R. O' Grady (Ed.), *Integrating service learning and multicultural education in colleges and universities* (pp. 45–58). New York: Routledge.

Devers, C. (2011). A critical pedagogy approach to online education: What we learned from a US/South African course. *Proceedings of Global Learning, 28,* 2199–2204.

Driscoll, A., Jicha, K., Hunt, A. N., Tichavsky, L., & Thompson, G. (2012). Can online courses deliver in-class results? A comparison of student performance and satisfaction in an online versus a face-to-face introductory sociology course. *Teaching Sociology, 40*, 312–331.

Eudey, B. (2012). Civic engagement, cyberfeminism, and online learning: Activism and service learning in women's and gender studies courses. *Feminist Teacher, 22*, 233–250.

Eyler, J. (2001). Creating your reflection map. *New Directions for Higher Education, 2001*(114), 35–43.

Gratton-Lavoie, C., & Stanley, D. (2009). Teaching and learning principles of microeconomics online: An empirical assessment. *Journal of Economic Education, 40*, 3–25.

Guthrie, K. L., & McCracken, H. (2010). Teaching and learning social justice through online service-learning courses. *International Review of Research in Open and Distributed Learning, 11*, 78–94.

Hannay, M., & Newvine, T. (2006). Perceptions of distance learning: A comparison of online and traditional learning. *Journal of Online Learning and Teaching, 2*, 1–11.

Howard, J. P. F. (1998). Academic service learning: A counternormative pedagogy. *New Directions for Teaching and Learning, 1998*(73), 21–29. Retrieved November 10, 2016, from doi:10.1002/tl.7303.

Jung, I., & Rha, I. (2000). Effectiveness and cost-effectiveness of online education: A review of the literature. *Educational Technology, 40*(4), 57–60.

Kiely, R. (2005). A transformative learning model for service-learning: A longitudinal case study. *Michigan Journal of Community Service Learning, 12*, 5–22.

Lack, K. A. (2013, March 21). Current status of research on online learning in postsecondary education. *Ithaka S + R, zuletzt geprüft am.* Retrieved October 20, 2016, from http://www.sr.ithaka.org/wp-content/uploads/2015/08/ithaka-sr-online-learning-postsecondary-education-may2012.pdf.

Levesque-Bristol, C., Knapp, T. D., & Fisher, B. J. (2010). The effectiveness of service-learning: It's not always what you think. *Journal of Experiential Education, 33*, 208–224.

Li, C.-S., & Irby, B. (2008). An overview of online education: Attractiveness, benefits, challenges, concerns and recommendations. *College Student Journal, 42*, 449–458.

McGorry, S. Y. (2012). No significant difference in service learning online. *Journal of Asynchronous Learning Networks, 16*(4), 45–54.

Mills, C. W. (2000). *The sociological imagination.* Oxford: Oxford University Press (original work published in 1959).

Mitchell, T. D. (2008). Traditional vs. critical service-learning: Engaging the literature to differentiate two models. *Michigan Journal of Community Service Learning, 14*(2), 50–65.

Mobley, C. (2007). Breaking ground engaging undergraduates in social change through service learning. *Teaching Sociology, 3*, 125–137.

Nguyen, T. (2015). The effectiveness of online learning: Beyond no significant difference and future horizons. *MERLOT Journal of Online Learning and Teaching, 11*, 309–319.

Parker-Gwin, R., & Mabry, J. B. (1998). Service learning as pedagogy and civic education: Comparing outcomes for three models. *Teaching Sociology, 26*, 276–291.

Petray, T., & Halbert, K. (2013). Teaching engagement: Reflections on sociological praxis. *Journal of Sociology, 49*, 441–455.

Putnam, R. D. (2001). *Bowling alone: The collapse and revival of American community.* New York: Simon and Schuster.

Radford, A. W., Cominole, M., & Skomsvold, P. (2015, September). Demographic and enrollment characteristics of nontraditional undergraduates: 2011–12. Report No.: NCES 2015-025. U.S. Department of Education. Retrieved November 10, 2016, from http://nces.ed.gov/pubsearch/pubsinfo.asp?pubid=2015025.

Ralph, B., & McNeal, J. R. (2012). Online versus traditional instruction: Quasi-experimental evidence from a college-level introduction to sociology course. *Indian Journal of Open Learning, 21*, 3–18.

Rose, S. (1989). The protest as a teaching technique for promoting feminist activism. *NWSA Journal, 1*, 486–490.

118 *Jin Young Choi*

Snyder, T. D., de Brey, C., & Dillow, S. A. (2016, April). Digest of education statistics 2014, NCES 2016–006. National Center for Education Statistics. Retrieved November 10, 2016, from http://nces.ed.gov/programs/digest/d14/tables/dt14_330.10.asp.

Stake, R. E. (2005). Qualitative case studies. In Norman K. Denzin & Yvonna S. Lincoln (Eds.), *The Sage handbook of qualitative research* (pp. 443–466). Thousand Oaks, CA: Sage.

Swords, A. C. S., & Kiely, R. (2010). Beyond pedagogy: Service learning as movement building in higher education. *Journal of Community Practice, 18*, 148–170.

Waldner, L. S., McGorry, S. Y., & Widener, M. C. (2012). E-service-learning: The evolution of service-learning to engage a growing online student population. *Journal of Higher Education Outreach and Engagement, 16*, 123–150.

Wang, Y., & Rodgers, R. (2006). Impact of service-learning and social justice education on college students' cognitive development." *NASPA Journal, 43*, 316–337.

Yin, R. K. (2013). *Case study research: Design and methods.* Thousand Oaks, CA: Sage.

*Chapter Nine*

# Academic Community Engagement Research in Kinesiology

*Undergraduate Students' Attitudes Toward Individuals with Disabilities*

## Jihyun Lee, José A. Santiago, Seung Ho Chang, and Justin A. Haegele

Academic community engagement is an instructional approach in higher education that offers undergraduate students the opportunity to learn knowledge and skills to meet course objectives while providing services to the community (Butin, 2010). This approach is based on experiential learning frameworks (e.g., Kolb's learning theory) that support the notion of knowledge developing through direct experience and transformation of such experience through reflection (Kolb, 1984). Thus, undergraduate students in courses that offer academic community engagement can effectively understand content while applying knowledge and theory to relevant practice and reflection on their own actions.

Various forms of academic community engagement exist, including volunteering, community service, community outreach, service learning, and internships. Among them, service learning is an academic community engagement method in which students (a) participate in service activities that are directly related to course objectives, (b) gain a better understanding of course content while building a sense of civic responsibility (Bringle & Hatcher, 1995), and (c) reflect to explore the impact on the self and the community (Scott & Graham, 2015).

These features of service learning differentiate it from other forms of academic community engagement. For instance, although volunteer activities may teach undergraduate students volunteerism or giving, it would not create reciprocity between the undergraduate student and community or directly support the student's learning to achieve course objectives.

Service-learning opportunities offer students both "serving to learn" and "learning to serve" experiences that meet academic course content and objectives (Bringle & Hatcher, 1995; Simon et al., 2013). A well-designed service-learning component utilized in an academic course can accelerate students' understanding of the content by leading them to apply their knowledge in practice.

Service learning as an instructional approach in higher education has been widely used in kinesiology (e.g., Bishop & Driver, 2007; Watson, Crandell, Hueglin, & Eisenman, 2002). In particular, adapted physical activity/adapted physical education (APA/APE) courses often take advantage of service learning. Typical service-learning formats that are used in APA/APE courses include physical activity programs where undergraduate students learn how to interact with individuals with disabilities in physical activity settings and develop, implement, and modify movement tasks to meet the needs of individuals with disabilities. In general, these programs use one of the following formats: (a) university or community based, (b) disability specific or individuals with disabilities in general, and (c) individuals with disabilities only or including both individuals with and without disabilities.

Understanding of research in service learning in a field including methodology and findings is important in order to determine what future research should address to contribute to the field. This chapter summarizes research findings about the effects of service-learning methodology on undergraduate kinesiology students' attitudes toward individuals with disabilities. Weaknesses of this area of research are addressed, and suggestions are provided for future research. Thus, this chapter will provide the rationale behind the service-learning methodology in APA/APE and serve as a useful guideline for future research topics. In addition, faculty teaching APA/APE courses may find the chapter beneficial in designing service-learning experiences for their students.

## SERVICE LEARNING IN ADAPTED PHYSICAL ACTIVITY/ EDUCATION COURSES

Many benefits of using service learning in APA/APE courses have been addressed. First, hands-on experiences during service learning can improve undergraduate student's attitudes toward individuals with disabilities and diversity awareness (e.g., Hardin, 2005; Miller, 2012; Roper & Santiago, 2014). Second, service learning can enhance undergraduate students' self-efficacy, self-esteem (Wade, 1995), and pedagogical content knowledge

(Meaney, Griffin, & Bohler, 2009). Third, undergraduate students can gain a deeper understanding of the APA/APE content through service learning than through traditional lecture formats (Strange, 2004).

One of the strengths of service learning is that it facilitates transfer of prior learning to new situations (Bringle & Hatcher, 1995). This feature of service learning is particularly effective to promote student learning in APA/APE because of the highly applied scientific nature of the field (Reid, 2000). The interlinkages between APA/APE and other disciplinary areas such as special education (e.g., Haegele, Lee, & Porretta, 2015; Lee & Haegele, 2015) creates a complexity of its knowledge structure. Thus, undergraduate students in APA/APE courses need to be exposed to more contextually specific learning environments where they have the opportunity to bridge the gap between theory and practice (LaMaster, 2001). It is essential to provide undergraduate students with multiple examples and learning opportunities to think critically and solve real-world problems (Meaney, Bohler, Kopf, Hernandez, & Scott, 2008).

Currently, empirical evidence on the use of service learning in APA/APE courses mainly focuses on its effects on undergraduate students' attitudes toward individuals with disabilities. Research suggests that the attitudes of physical education teachers are central to the learning experiences of children with disabilities (Block & Obrusnikova, 2007; Haegele, Zhu, & Davis, 2016; Li & Chen, 2012). The extant literature provides illustrations, from the perspectives of students with disabilities, of how teacher attitudes can influence their physical education experiences through discrimination and exclusionary actions (Bredahl, 2013; Coates, 2012; Haegele & Sutherland, 2015).

The following section describes research in two different areas: (1) research findings pertaining to attitudes toward individuals with disabilities and teaching those with disabilities, and (2) the influence of contextual factors related to the influence of service-learning research in kinesiology.

## RESEARCH FINDINGS FROM PREVIOUS APA/APE SERVICE-LEARNING RESEARCH

### Changes in Attitudes

Several studies have explored general attitudinal change as a result of service-learning approaches in APA/APE courses (e.g., Rowe & Stutts, 1987; Santiago, Lee, & Roper, 2016; Stewart, 1990), and findings have been inconsistent. Although Rowe and Stutts (1987) and Stewart (1990) reported positive changes in attitudes of undergraduate kinesiology students after service-learning experiences, the results from Santiago et al. (2016), who used a university campus–based APA/APE service-learning program (one session per week over six weeks, with 55 minutes per session), did not support previous studies.

Santiago and colleagues attributed the lack of significant influence to the quality and quantity of the undergraduate students' contact time with the children with disabilities during the service-learning experience. They concluded that the service-learning experience was too short in time and failed to create an environment of equal status between the undergraduate students and children with disabilities to produce attitude change. Furthermore, Santiago et al. suggested that in order to influence attitudinal change positively, it is important to consider the quality and quantity of contact time with individuals with disabilities when designing service-learning experiences in APA/APE courses.

As the inclusion of children with disabilities in physical education gained more acceptance (Block, 1999), APA/APE researchers shifted their interests from general attitudes to attitudes related to teaching. Although some physical education and APE teachers were supportive of inclusion (Casebolt & Hodge, 2010; Sato, Hodge, Murata, & Maeda, 2007), they are often concerned about their ability to deliver quality instruction in inclusive physical education (Hodge et al., 2009).

Research suggests that teachers' attitudes are closely associated with self-efficacy, pre-service training, and experience in teaching students with disabilities (e.g., Block & Rizzo, 1995; Rizzo & Vispoel, 1992). Thus, providing additional opportunities for undergraduate students to work directly with individuals with disabilities may result in improved self-efficacy and consequently develop more favorable attitudes toward teaching students with disabilities. Studies have shown that service learning in APA/APE courses can improve attitudes of physical education–major students toward teaching students with disabilities in physical education (e.g., Folsom-Meek, Nearing, & Kalakian, 2000; Hodge & Jansma, 1999; Hodge, Tannehill, & Kluge, 2003; Rizzo & Vispoel, 1991).

## Contextual Factors of APA/APE Service Learning

Studies have examined how various contextual factors of service learning employed in APA/APE courses would change undergraduate students' attitudes toward individuals with disabilities. Those contextual factors can be categorized into the following: (a) types and location of service learning, (b) gender of undergraduate students, (c) undergraduate students' previous experiences with individuals with disabilities, and (d) participants' disability types.

## Types and Location of Service Learning

Rowe and Stutts (1987) and Stewart (1990) examined different APA/APE program types and attitudes of physical education undergraduate students toward individuals with disabilities. In each of these studies, undergraduate students participated in various service-learning experience contexts (e.g., motor development program for children with disabilities, adapted swimming programs). Results from both studies revealed that physical education undergraduate students' attitudes were improved as a result of the service-learning experience regardless of the type of the APA/APE program employed.

Only one group of undergraduate students in Stewart (1990) who participated in the swimming program for elderly participants did not show such results. Rowe and Stutts (1987) suggest that "hands on" experiences are critical and should be systematically integrated into APA/APE courses. However, Stewart cautioned that exposure to individuals with disabilities alone may not influence attitudinal change and suggested close attention to the structure and design of the service-learning experience.

Several studies have also explored the effects of the location of the service-learning experience on undergraduate students' attitudes toward teaching students with disabilities. For example, Hodge and Jansma (1999) examined the attitudes of undergraduate students who had on-campus or off-campus service-learning experience at weeks 1, 10, and 15 during an introductory APE course. Results revealed significantly higher attitude scores in both locations in weeks 10 and 15 compared to the first week.

Both on-campus and off-campus service-learning experiences with individuals with disabilities positively influenced undergraduate students' attitudes toward teaching individuals with disabilities. However, the attitudes of undergraduate students who had on-campus experience were significantly higher than undergraduate students who had off-campus experience. Hodge and Jansma (1999) attributed this finding to the close supervision provided to the students with disabilities and larger undergraduate students–children ratios during the on-campus compared to the off-campus service-learning program.

Hodge, Davis, Woodard, and Sherrill (2002) also compared the effects of on-campus and off-campus APA/APE service-learning experiences on undergraduate physical education students' attitudes and perceived competence in teaching students with disabilities. The on-campus experience consisted of four different types of activity programs while the off-campus consisted of a self-contained physical education program at a local elementary school.

Unlike Hodge and Jansma (1999), no significant differences were found between the two types of service-learning experiences. Hodge et al. (2002)

attributed the lack of attitudinal change to several factors: (a) lack of autonomy by the APE course instructor over programmatic decisions of the service-learning experience and (b) teaching philosophy and content selection of the APE course instructor not specifically structured to cause attitudinal change. These findings indicate the need for careful planning and consideration of the quality of the service-learning experience.

Most recently, Rust and Sinelnikov (2010) qualitatively explored the perceptions of a pre-service physical education teacher in a self-contained environment during an on-campus service-learning experience. This case study revealed that the participant thought that on-campus experience may have been misguided in its structure. The participant stated, "I wish I would have had . . . four or five students (with disabilities), you know, because when you go out to schools, it's not going to be just one-on-one. It'll be like one-on-ten, or whatever the case may be" (Rust & Sinelnikov, 2010, pp. 37–38).

The recommendations from this study include providing a more realistic teaching scenario during field experiences. Further, results from this study suggested that multiple courses in APE are needed to develop a deeper understanding of how to teach students with various disabilities (Rust & Sinelnikov, 2010).

Although studies have explored how the type or location of APA/APE service learning affects attitudes of undergraduate students toward teaching individuals with disabilities, there is insufficient evidence to support a particular format of service learning in APA/APE courses. In most cases, the format of service learning in APA/APE courses is chosen by the faculty member for convenience. Factors such as local school campus availability, scheduled time of the APA/APE course offered, and existing program in place drive the selection of the service-learning format rather than evidence-based reasons.

## Gender of Undergraduate Students

Researchers have hypothesized that the gender of undergraduate students would play an important role in determining more favorable attitudes toward teaching individuals with disabilities after service learning. However, results from previous studies are inconclusive. Santiago et al. (2016) reported that there were no significant main or interaction effects for gender as the majority of previous studies demonstrated (i.e., Hodge & Jansma, 1999; Rowe & Stutts, 1987). However, Folsom-Meek, Nearing, Groteluschen, and Krampf (1999) found more favorable attitudes among female than male undergraduate students.

*Previous Experience with Individuals with Disabilities*

Santiago et al. (2016) found a negative correlation ($r$ = -0.13) between kine-siology students' attitudes and prior contact with individuals with disabil-ities. They argued that previous experiences of the participants of their study may not have been positive or of quality. As a result, this may have made their attitudes difficult to change even after the service-learning experience. Even though the quality and types of contact were not examined, the results of Santiago et al. may serve as meaningful evidence that only quality experi-ences such as meaningful and pleasant interactions with individuals with disabilities (e.g., Sherrill, Heikinaro-Johanson, & Slininger, 1994) result in favorable attitudes.

Past negative experiences with individuals with disabilities may increase the potential for stereotypical and preconceived beliefs of undergraduate stu-dents even after service learning (Santiago et al., 2016). Roper and Santiago (2014) argued that undergraduate kinesiology students in their study ex-pressed stress and anxiety prior to their service-learning experience. These feelings of the undergraduate students in their study seemed to be dissipated during and after they interacted with the students with disabilities in their service learning. It is not conclusive whether this anxiety and stress are related to their previous experience with individuals with disabilities, and future research can explore this area.

*Disability Type*

Consensus exists that the disability type of the student could affect the atti-tudes of in-service and pre-service physical education teachers (e.g., Rizzo & Kirkendall, 1995). Even though disability variables were not explored in Santiago et al. (2016) and Roper and Santiago (2014), an extensive line of research has provided evidence that physical educators tend to have more favorable attitudes toward teaching students with less severe disabilities (i.e., Rizzo, 1984; Rizzo & Vispoel, 1991; Rizzo & Wright, 1987; Schmidt-Gotz, Doll-Tepper, & Lienert, 1994; Tripp, 1988).

One possible explanation is that physical education teachers may have low perceived competence in their ability to provide effective instruction for students with severe disabilities. Block and Rizzo (1995) reported that physi-cal education teachers are underprepared to provide quality education for students with severe, multiple disabilities. Thus, the disability type may play a role as a mediator in increasing or decreasing the effects of service learning on physical education–major students' attitudes toward teaching students with disabilities.

Most recently, Sato and Haegele (2016) described and explained the ex-periences pre-service teachers had instructing students with severe and pro-found disabilities during course-related service-learning experiences in schools. Among their findings, participants reported a "reality shock" when students with severe and profound disabilities demonstrated unpredictable or unusual behaviors. Many of the pre-service teachers in this study had had previous teaching experiences with children with disabilities; however, this was the first time they had taught students with severe and profound disabilities, and they were not expecting the magnitude or frequency of unpredictable behaviors. Participants in this study suggested that service-learning experiences should include more specific behavior management orientations that could help prepare them for these types of experiences.

## WEAKNESSES OF APA/APE SERVICE-LEARNING RESEARCH AND FUTURE RESEARCH

While studies indicate positive effects of service learning on undergraduate students' general attitudes as well as attitudes toward teaching students with disabilities (e.g., Hodge & Jansma, 1999; Hodge et al., 2002; Rizzo & Vispoel, 1992), several limitations of this line of research exist. In this section, issues related to methodology and outcome measures of previous studies are described in order to provide suggestions for future research.

First, the construct of attitude and instruments used to assess it need to be considered. The concept of attitude is highly complex and situational (Antonak & Livneh, 2000; Findler, Vilchinsky, & Werner, 2007). For instance, Santiago et al. (2016), when trying to understand why there was a lack of change in attitudinal scores in the ATDP-Form A scale (Yuker, Block, & Younng, 1970) after a service-learning experience, indicated that the ATDP scale was a unidimensional measure of attitudes and may have failed in detecting other important attitudinal components (e.g., behavioral, affective, or cognitive). On the contrary, a qualitative study conducted by Roper and Santiago (2014) using a similar service-learning experience resulted in positive attitudinal change toward school-age children with disabilities. This may indicate that qualitative methodology was able to capture the study participants' attitudinal changes that were not detected by the ATDP scale in Santiago et al. (2016).

A second issue is centered around the use of theoretical frameworks in this line of research that can drive the design and structure of service learning as an independent variable. Previous studies in this area have been grounded in various theories such as contact theory (e.g., Santiago et al., 2016) and TRA (Rizzo & Vispoel, 1991). However, researchers often paid less attention to creating strong connections between theories and how service learning was designed in a study. For example, if contact theory is used, the service-learning experience should be designed using the four conditions suggested by Allport (1954), including equal status, intimate rather than casual, interactive and pleasant, and focused on common goals. However, often pre-structured service-learning experiences are used and the four conditions of contact theory are compromised.

One theoretical framework that has been recently used (Sato & Haegele, 2016) and may provide important insight is occupational socialization theory (Lawson, 1983). Occupational socialization is a theoretical framework that guides researchers in understanding why teachers think about and teach the way they do (Stran & Curtner-Smith, 2009). While this framework has been thoroughly explored in the way the physical education profession trains teachers (e.g., Curtner-Smith & Sofo, 2004; Lawson, 1983), few studies have used it to explore the effectiveness of service-learning experiences in APE (Sato & Haegele, 2016).

A third limitation of the extant literature is that the perspective of students with disabilities participating in the service-learning experience has been absent (Haegele & Sutherland, 2015). Exploring this perspective can provide important insight into the effectiveness of the pre-service physical education teachers participating in the experience as well as attitudes toward those teachers' abilities. Furthermore, future research may consider exploring both the pre-service teacher's and the student's perspective toward the experience in one context to find a more global understanding of the dynamics within the experience (Haegele & Sutherland, 2015).

Lastly, limited outcome variables have been used, and this has provided evidence on a narrow scope of the benefits of service learning in APA/APE in higher education. The majority of studies have mainly focused on undergraduate students' attitudinal changes because of their service-learning experience. However, other potential outcome variables can provide valuable information about the impact of service learning, such as (a) actual behavioral changes of physical education undergraduate students (e.g., instructional behaviors, interactions with students with disabilities); (b) experiences of other service-learning participants (e.g., parents of children with disabilities); (c) student-faculty relationships (Chabot & Holben, 2003); and (d) the influence on their career choice. This line of research can provide evidence on service learning as a better instructional approach to assist undergraduate students in achieving more success in APA/APE courses than a traditional instructional method.

## CONCLUSION

Service learning is used in many higher education kinesiology programs. In particular, APA/APE courses typically offer an on- or off-campus field experience working directly with children and youth with disabilities. Research has demonstrated that undergraduate students in kinesiology can gain much-

128     *Jihyun Lee, José A. Santiago, Seung Ho Chang, and Justin A. Haegele*

needed practical experience and improve attitudes toward individuals with disabilities through service learning.

This chapter introduces research findings on the influence of service learning on undergraduate kinesiology students' attitudes toward individuals with disabilities from a research perspective. Previously published research has been briefly reviewed and general findings and limitations of this line of research were addressed. Overall, studies found that service learning is beneficial in improving attitudes toward individuals with disabilities. Despite some weaknesses, however, adopting service-learning methodology in an undergraduate APA/APE course is valuable. Future research should address how service learning influences undergraduate students' knowledge and skills and the quality of life of individuals with disabilities in the community.

## REFERENCES

Allport, G. W. (1954). *The nature of prejudice*. Cambridge, MA: Perseus Books.
Antonak, R. F., & Livneh, H. (2000). Measurement of attitudes towards persons with disabilities. *Disability and Rehabilitation, 22*(5), 211–224.
Bishop, J., & Driver, S. (2007). Implementing service-learning in undergraduate adapted physical education. *Journal of Physical Education, Recreation & Dance, 78*(8), 15–19.
Block, M. E. (1999). Did we jump on the wrong bandwagon? Problems with inclusion in physical education. *Palaestra, 15*(3), 30–36, 55–56.
Block, M. E., & Obrusnikova, I. (2007). Inclusion in physical education: A review of literature from 1995–2005. *Adapted Physical Activity Quarterly, 24*(2), 103–124.
Block, M. E., & Rizzo, T. L. (1995). Attitudes and attributes associated with teaching individuals with severe and profound disabilities. *Journal of the Association for Persons with Severe Handicaps, 20*(1), 80–87.
Bredahl, A. M. (2013). Sitting and watching the others being active: The experienced difficulties in physical education when having a disability. *Adapted Physical Activity Quarterly, 30*(1), 40–58.
Bringle, R. G., & Hatcher, J. A. (1995). A service learning curriculum for faculty. *Michigan Journal of Community Service-Learning, 2*(1), 112–122.
Butin, D. (2010). *Service-learning in theory and practice*. New York: Palgrave Macmillan.
Casebolt, K. M., & Hodge, S. R. (2010). High school physical education teachers' beliefs about teaching students with mild to severe disabilities. *Physical Educator, 67*(3), 140–156.
Chabot, J. M., & Holben, D. H. (2003). Integrating service-learning into dietetics and nutrition education. *Topics in Clinical Nutrition, 18*(3), 177–184.
Coates, J. (2012). Teaching inclusively: Are secondary physical education student teachers sufficiently prepared to teach in inclusive environments? *Physical Education and Sport Pedagogy, 17*(4), 349–365.
Curtner-Smith, M. D., & Sofo, S. (2004). Preservice teachers' conceptions of teaching with sport education and multi-activity units. *Sport Education and Society, 9*(3), 347–377.
Findler, L., Vilchinsky, N., & Werner, S. (2007). The Multidimensional Attitudes Scale toward persons with disabilities (MAS): Construction and validation. *Rehabilitation Counseling Bulletin, 50*(3), 166–176.
Folsom-Meek, S. L., Nearing, R. J., Groteluschen, W., & Krampf, H. (1999). Effects of academic major, gender, and hands-on experience on attitudes of preservice professionals. *Adapted Physical Activity Quarterly, 16*(4), 389–402.
Folsom-Meek, S. L., Nearing, R. J., & Kalakian, L. (2000). Effects of an adapted physical education course in changing attitudes. *Clinical Kinesiology, 54*(3), 52–58.

Haegele, J. A., Lee, J., & Porretta, D. L. (2015). Research trends in *Adapted Physical Activity Quarterly* from 2004 to 2013. *Adapted Physical Activity Quarterly, 32*(3), 187–205.

Haegele, J. A., & Sutherland, S. (2015). The perspective of students with disabilities toward physical education: A review of qualitative inquiry. *Quest, 67*(3), 255–273.

Haegele, J. A., Zhu, X., & Davis, S. (2016). The meaning of physical education and sport among elite athletes with visual impairments. *European Physical Education Review.* Epub ahead of print, May 26, 2016: doi:10.1177/1356336X16650122.

Hardin, B. (2005). Physical education teachers' reflections on preparation for inclusion. *Physical Educator, 62*(1), 44–56.

Hodge, S. R., Ammah, J. O. A., Casebolt, K. M., LaMaster, K., Hersman, B. L., Samalot-Rivera, A., & Sato, T. (2009). A diversity of voices: Physical education teachers' beliefs on teaching students with disabilities. *International Journal of Disability, Development and Education, 56*(4), 401–419.

Hodge, S. R., Davis, R., Woodard, R., & Sherrill, C. (2002). Comparison of practicum types in changing preservice teachers' attitudes and perceived competence. *Adapted Physical Activity Quarterly, 19*(2), 155–171.

Hodge, S. R., & Jansma, P. (1999). Effects of contact time and location of practicum experiences on attitudes of physical education majors. *Adapted Physical Activity Quarterly, 16*(1), 48–63.

Hodge, S. R., Tannehill, D., & Kluge, M. (2003). Exploring the meaning of practicum experiences for PETE students. *Adapted Physical Activity Quarterly, 20*(4), 381–390.

Kolb, D. (1984). *Experiential learning: Experience as the source of learning and development.* Englewood Cliffs, NJ: Prentice Hall.

LaMaster, K. (2001). Enhancing preservice teachers field experiences through the addition of a service-learning component. *Journal of Experiential Education, 24*(1), 27–33.

Lawson, H. A. (1983). Toward a model of teacher socialization in physical education: The subjective warrant, recruitment, and teacher education (part 1). *Journal of Teaching in Physical Education, 2*(3), 3–16.

Lee, J., & Haegele, J. A. (2015). A cross-disciplinary comparison of publication trends: Adapted physical activity and special education. *European Journal of Adapted Physical Activity, 8*(1), 7–20.

Li, C., & Chen, S. (2012). Exploring experiences of physical activity in special school students with cerebral palsy: A qualitative perspective. *European Journal of Adapted Physical Activity, 5*(1), 7–17.

Meaney, K. S., Bohler, H. R., Kopf, K., Hernandez, L., & Scott, L. S. (2008). Service-learning and pre-service educators' cultural competence for teaching: An exploratory study. *Journal of Experiential Education, 31*(2), 189–208.

Meaney, K. S., Griffin, K., & Bohler, H. (2009). Service-learning: A venue for enhancing pre-service educators' knowledge base for teaching. *International Journal for the Scholarship of Teaching and Learning, 3*(2), 1–17.

Miller, M. (2012). The role of service-learning to promote early childhood physical education while examining its influence upon the vocational call to teach. *Physical Education and Sport Pedagogy, 17*(1), 61–77.

Reid, G. (2000). Future directions of inquiry in adapted physical activity. *Quest, 52*(4), 369–381.

Rizzo, T. L. (1984). Attitudes of physical educators toward teaching handicapped pupils. *Adapted Physical Activity Quarterly, 1*(4), 267–274.

Rizzo, T., & Kirkendall, D. (1995). Teaching students with mild disabilities: What affects attitudes of future physical educators? *Adapted Physical Activity Quarterly, 12*, 205–216.

Rizzo, T. L., & Vispoel, W. P. (1991). Physical educators' attitudes and attributes toward teaching students with handicaps. *Adapted Physical Activity Quarterly, 8*(1), 4–11.

Rizzo, T. L., & Vispoel, W. P. (1992). Changing attitudes about teaching students with handicaps. *Adapted Physical Activity Quarterly, 9*(1), 54–63.

Rizzo, T. L., & Wright, R. G. (1987). Secondary school physical educators' attitudes toward teaching students with handicaps. *American Corrective Therapy Journal, 41*(2), 52–55.

Roper, E. A., & Santiago, J. A. (2014). The influence of service learning on kinesiology students' attitudes toward P–12 students with disabilities. *Adapted Physical Activity Quarterly, 31*(2), 162–180. doi:10.1123/apaq.2013-0086.

Rowe, J., & Stutts, R. M. (1987). Effects of practica type, experience, and gender on attitudes of undergraduate physical education majors toward disabled persons. *Adapted Physical Activity Quarterly, 4*(4), 268–277.

Rust, R., & Sinelnikov, O. (2010). Practicum in a self-contained environment: Pre-service teacher perceptions of teaching students with disabilities. *The Physical Educator, 67*(1), 33–45.

Santiago, J. A., Lee, J., & Roper, E. A. (2016). Effects of service learning on kinesiology students' attitudes toward children with disabilities. *Journal of Higher Education Outreach and Engagement, 20*(2), 109–126.

Sato, T., & Haegele, J. A. (2016). Graduate students' practicum experiences instructing students with severe and profound disabilities in physical education. *European Physical Education Review.* Epub ahead of print, April 12, 2016: doi:10.1177/1356336X16642717.

Sato, T., Hodge, S., Murata, N., & Maeda, J. (2007). Japanese physical education teachers' beliefs about teaching students with disabilities. *Sport Education and Society, 12*(2), 211–230.

Schmidt-Gotz, E., Doll-Tepper, G., & Lienert, C. (1994). Attitudes of university students and teachers towards integrating students with disabilities in regular physical education classes. *Physical Education Review, 17*(1), 43–57.

Scott, K., & Graham, J. (2015). Service-learning: Implications for empathy and community engagement in elementary school children. *Journal of Experiential Education, 38*(4), 354–372.

Sherrill, C., Heikinaro-Johansson, P. M., & Slininger, D. (1994). Equal-status relationships in the gym. *Journal of Physical Education, Recreation and Dance, 65*(1), 27–31.

Simon, G. L., Wee, B. S. C., Chin, A., Tindle, A. D., Guth, D., & Mason, H. (2013). Synthesis for the interdisciplinary environmental sciences: Integrating systems approaches and service learning. *Journal of College Science Teaching, 42*(5), 42–49.

Stewart, C. C. (1990). Effect of practica types in preservice adapted physical education curriculum on attitudes toward disabled populations. *Journal of Teaching in Physical Education, 10*(1), 76–83.

Stran, M., & Curtner-Smith, M. (2009). Influence of occupational socialization on two preservice teachers' interpretation and delivery of the Sport Education Model. *Journal of Teaching in Physical Education, 28*(1), 38–53.

Strange, A. (2004). Long-term academic benefits of service-learning: When and where do they manifest themselves? *College Student Journal, 38*(2), 257–261.

Tripp, A. (1988). Comparison of attitudes of regular and adapted physical educators toward disabled individuals. *Perceptual Motor Skills, 66*(2), 425–426.

Wade, R. C. (1995). Developing active citizens: Community service-learning in social studies teacher education. *Social Studies, 86*(3), 122–128.

Watson, D. L., Crandell, J., Hueglin, S., & Eisenman, P. (2002). Incorporating service-learning into physical education teacher education programs. *Journal of Physical Education, Recreation & Dance, 73*(5), 50–55.

Yuker, H. E., Block, J. R., & Younng, J. H. (1970). *The measurement of attitudes toward disabled persons.* Albertson, NY: INA Mend Institute at Human Resources Center.

# Index

physical education, 21, 26, 120, 122, 123, 124, 125, 127
play therapy, 71–82
Play Therapy Consumer Satisfaction Survey (PTCSS), 74–82
political apathy, 1, 2, 3, 11
political efficacy, 2, 3, 6, 8, 9, 11, 11–12
political engagement, 1, 2, 3–4, 7
political interest, 3
political science, 2, 3, 11
pre-service teachers (PSTs), 43–55, 57–69, 86–97
professional identity, 85, 86, 88–89, 93–94, 96
professional socialization, 85
public administration, 3, 11

race, 5, 8–9, 11, 15, 59, 86, 106
rally, 5, 6, 7
reflection, 16, 17, 24, 28, 44, 47–48, 50, 53, 54, 59–60, 62, 73, 80, 81, 85, 91, 92, 94, 96, 105, 106, 107, 108

Sam Houston State University, 4, 11, 17, 32, 34, 61
school-to-prison pipeline, 15
sense of community (SOC), 88, 103

service learning, 2, 16, 32, 33, 43, 44–45, 57, 85, 88, 101–102, 103–105, 109–115, 119–120; definition, 2, 16, 60; international service learning (ISL), 85–97
social class, 28, 59, 106
social justice, 34, 58, 60, 60–61, 63, 66, 67, 74, 96, 115
social work, 45, 46
sociology, 102, 104, 106, 109–110, 113–114
Student Leadership, Thoughtful Service, Authentic Learning, Reflective Practice, Substantive Partnerships (STARS model), 17
study abroad, 85, 86, 86–87, 96

Teaching English to speakers of other languages (TESOL), 87, 88, 89, 90, 91, 97
transformative learning, 86
Twitter, 5, 6, 8

University of Houston-Downtown, 45, 48
urban education, 43, 45, 46

victimology, 31–41
vote, 2–3, 5, 6, 7, 8

# About the Editor and Contributors

**Heather K. Evans** is an associate professor of political science at Sam Houston State University. She has a Ph.D. from Indiana University, Bloomington, and a B.A. from Berea College. Her research interests include American politics, particularly public opinion, competitive elections, political communication, social media, the status of women in the discipline, Congress, and the effect of entertainment media on political attitudes. Her research has appeared in journals like *American Politics Research*, *PS: Political Science and Politics*, *Electoral Studies*, and the *Journal of Elections, Public Opinion, and Parties*. She is the author of *Competitive Elections and Democracy in America: The Good, the Bad, and the Ugly* (2014).

She also works with the Center for Community Engagement at Sam Houston State University and has received grants while at SHSU to investigate the effects of service learning on the political attitudes and behavior of undergraduate students.

\* \* \*

**Burcu Ates** is an assistant professor of bilingual/ESL education in the Department of Language Literacy and Special Populations at Sam Houston State University. Her research interests include pre- and in-service teacher professional development, international service learning, non-native English-speaking professionals, and World Englishes. She can be reached at ates@shsu.edu.

**James G. Booker** leads and directs Adult Protective Services operations in Houston, Texas. He has over 20 years of experience managing state agency operations that provide protective and social services to vulnerable older adults. Dr. Booker also co-directs the Texas Elder Abuse Mistreatment Institute, a multidisciplinary collaboration with the University of Texas Medical School, the Harris County hospital district, and other community agencies committed to improving the lives of mistreated older adults through clinical care, education, and research. He is a frequent speaker who has provided training and elder mistreatment education to students, service providers, and medical professionals. Dr. Booker's past research includes examining and developing undergraduate social science programs in the Houston area to include elder mistreatment curricula. James holds a B.A. in ethnic studies, an M.A. in sociology, and a Ph.D. in educational leadership.

**Mary M. Breaux** is a clinical assistant professor in the Department of Criminal Justice and Criminology at Sam Houston State University. Her area of expertise is victimology with a focus on child and elder maltreatment. Dr. Breaux serves as a member of the University of Texas Health Science Center Consortium on Aging and the Texas Elder Abuse Mistreatment Institute, and she is affiliated with the Criminal Justice Center Crime Victims' Institute. Prior to accepting a full-time faculty position, Dr. Breaux worked nearly 20 years with the Texas Department of Family and Protective Services gaining practical experience in areas such as community relations (Adult Protective Services), case management (Child Protective Services), training, and human resources.

**Rick Bruhn** is a professor of counselor education at Sam Houston State University. He is also a psychotherapist and family therapist in private practice. Dr. Bruhn started his study of play therapy and consultation with Head Start programs in the 1970s. He has been offering Academic Community Engagement counseling internship classes since 2013.

**Seung Ho Chang** is an assistant professor in the Department of Kinesiology at San Jose State University. He earned his Ph.D. in kinesiology with a specialization in motor development and physical education teacher education from The Ohio State University, Columbus, Ohio. Dr. Chang's research agenda focuses on two complementary areas: motor development and physical education teacher education. His primary research area is the motor competence and physical activity of disadvantaged preschoolers with developmental delays. The intent of this research is to understand the complex interactions of multiple subsystems from the task, environment, and child in order to develop and implement high-quality motor skill interventions in schools, communities, and families. His second line of research is to identify the types of teachers' content knowledge (CK) and pedagogical content knowledge (PCK) and how CK and PCK play a significant role in promoting students' fundamental motor skills in physical education class.

**Jin Young Choi** is associate professor in the Department of Sociology at Sam Houston State University. Based on her interdisciplinary academic training in sociology and public health, her research has focused on immigrant and minority health and health policy, the nutrition transition and dietary change, obesity, and occupational health in the food industry. She has published in a number of leading journals and books in the social sciences, health, and food studies. Dr. Choi also has a wealth of experience with various minority populations and rural communities through her professional and service activities. Her research and community experience is a powerful driver of her passion for service-learning courses. She has developed and taught service-learning classes since 2011.

**Colin Dalton** is an assistant professor of literacy education and TESOL in the Department of Urban Education at the University of Houston–Downtown, Texas. His teaching and research interests include literacy development and practice utilizing alternate texts to develop lifelong readers. Dr. Dalton first earned a B.A. from the University of Oregon and then completed his M.Ed. and Ed.D. degrees at the University of Houston. He may be reached at daltonc@uhd.edu.

**Yvonne Garza-Chaves** received her Ph.D. in counselor education from the University of North Texas with a specialty in play therapy. She is currently an associate professor, and her current service posts include internship coordinator, as well as coordinator of the Play Therapy Institute in the Department of Counselor Education at Sam Houston State University in Huntsville, Texas. She has over 20 years of clinical experience working with children and families in the areas of both outpatient and inpatient mental health, including work with juvenile offenders, children and adolescents in schools, and contract work with cancer patients. She is active in the professional community and has served on the board of the local and state play therapy associations and is on several committees for the national play therapy association.

**Barbara Greybeck** is a retired professor, formerly in the Department of Language, Literacy, and Special Populations at Sam Houston State University in Huntsville, Texas. She has worked extensively to engage graduate and undergraduate students in service-learning experiences related to education and has also served on the steering committee for Academic Community Engagement at the university level.

**Yurimi Grigsby** is an associate professor of ESL education in the Department of Teaching, Learning, and Diversity at Concordia University Chicago.

Previously, she was a high school Spanish and ESL teacher in Tennessee. Her current work focuses on language education and language varieties of marginalized communities.

**Justin A. Haegele** is an assistant professor in the Department of Human Movement Sciences at Old Dominion University. He is an accomplished young scholar in adapted physical education and has published numerous articles in national/international physical education and disability-related academic journals, as well as a number of textbook chapters. In recent years, Justin has been the recipient of Research Fellow status with the Society of Health and Physical Educators (SHAPE America), the 2015 David P. Beaver Adapted Physical Activity Young Scholar Award (National Consortium for Physical Education for Individuals with Disabilities), and the New York State Adapted Physical Education Teacher of the Year Award in 2012 (New York State Association for Health, Physical Education, Recreation, & Dance). His scholarly interests include physical activity participation, including in physical education, of individuals with visual impairments; physical education and physical activity experiences of individuals with autism spectrum disorder; and inclusion in physical education and physical activity settings.

**Richard C. Henriksen Jr.** is a professor of counselor education at Sam Houston State University. He has worked with children in Discipline Alternative Education Programs for more than 20 years and has been involved with service learning for more than 15 years. Dr. Henriksen's research interests include working with children who have difficulty in traditional education environments.

**John Kelly** is an associate professor in the Department of Urban Education at the University of Houston–Downtown, Texas. He teaches a number of online/hybrid special education and classroom assessment courses that are designed to address the needs of the neo-millennial learning styles of future urban general educators. In addition, he provides instruction in graduate-level education research. He received his undergraduate degree from Rice University, his masters from Prairie View A&M University, and a Ph.D. from the University of Texas at Austin where he focused on learning disabilities, behavior disorders, and developmental disabilities. His primary research interest is studying the impact of self-determination on LD/BD and PDD populations. In addition, he has a personal interest (a 26-year-old son and a 7-year-old grandson) in autism and developmental disabilities. Prior to entering the education field, he spent 30 years in the financial services industry.

**Jihyun Lee** is an assistant professor in the Department of Kinesiology at San Jose State University, California. Her research explores adapted physical activity/education service-learning effects on undergraduate students' perception and instructional behavior, mechanisms underlying the effects of physical activity on motor development of children with disabilities, and fitness and health-related quality of life for adults with disabilities. Her research has focused on community-based intervention programs such as movement-based social skills programs for children with autism and a fitness program for youth with disabilities in community-based transition programs. She has written book chapters, published articles, and presented at state, national, and international conferences on these topics.

**Diane M. Miller** is an assistant professor of literacy in the Department of Urban Education at the University of Houston–Downtown, Texas. In addition to preparing pre-service teachers and graduate students in the area of English, language arts, and reading, she pursues her research interests of content-area literacy instruction, adolescent literacy, bridging research to practice, and hybrid learning environments. Dr. Miller earned a B.A. from the University of Texas at Austin, an M.A. from Texas A&M University–Texarkana, and a Ph.D. from Texas A&M University at College Station. She may be reached at petersond@uhd.edu.

**Judith A. Nelson** retired as an associate professor from Sam Houston State University in the Counselor Education Department in 2015 and is currently living in Tucson, Arizona. She is licensed as a professional counselor in Texas and Arizona and continues to be involved in the counseling profession as an adjunct at Sam Houston and serves on the School Counseling Advisory Board at the University of Arizona. In addition, she is the sole proprietor of Nelson Consulting and conducts program evaluations, provides consultation and training, and presents workshops on a number of topics. Dr. Nelson worked as a professional school counselor for more than 20 years and received grant money to establish service learning programs at alternative schools in Houston, Texas.

**Denise Peterson** earned her Ph.D. from the Counselor Education Program at Sam Houston State University. Dr. Peterson is currently director of clinical services at Scotty's House, a child advocacy center in Bryan, Texas, and an adjunct professor with Sam Houston State University. She is a licensed professional counselor-supervisor in the state of Texas and is a registered play therapist-supervisor. She has worked in a private practice, university clinic, and school settings where she provided counseling services for children, adolescents, and their families on a variety of issues. In addition to using the office setting to provide services, she has been actively engaged in providing counseling in non-traditional settings. In addition to providing trauma-informed counseling services to children and their families, she provides supervision for counseling interns and play therapists.

**Mary A. Petrón** is an associate professor of bilingual/ESL in the Department of Language, Literacy, and Special Populations at Sam Houston State University. Her research interests include ESL teacher education, U.S.-Mexico transnationalism, and context-specific language education.

**José A. Santiago** is an associate professor in the Department of Kinesiology at Sam Houston State University. His primary research focuses on the examination of physical education teachers' content knowledge of health-related fitness. Santiago earned his Ed.D. from Texas Southern University.

**Baburhan Uzum** is an assistant professor of bilingual/ESL in the Department of Language, Literacy, and Special Populations at Sam Houston State University. His research interests include multicultural teacher education, service learning/academic community engagement initiatives in teacher education, and interculturality in language learning and teaching.

www.ingramcontent.com/pod-product-compliance
Lightning Source LLC
Chambersburg PA
CBHW021820270326
41932CB00007B/270